Why the Rich Stay Rich
and the Poor Stay Poor

by Mark Prather
edited by Courtney Prather

Acknowledgments

The message in this book is the accumulation of life lessons that many people have contributed to over the years. These lessons are more than financial- they include lessons of compassion, integrity, and faith, to name a few.

I would first like to thank my parents for their determination to keep a roof over our family during some very difficult financial times in my childhood. I would also like to acknowledge the blessing that growing up in an inner-city environment has been to my life. Understanding the challenges and demands placed on the people living in this environment has inspired me to make a difference in the lives of those facing these challenges. Lastly, I would like to thank my family for all of their love and support, my wife Mary, sons Brice, Chasin and Blaine, and especially my daughter Courtney for joining me on this project.

Table of Contents

Chapter One
Belief Systems

"Understand that to achieve anything requires faith and belief in yourself, vision, hard work, determination, and dedication. Remember, all things are possible for those who believe."

-Gail Devers, three-time Olympic champion track and field athlete, survivor of Graves' disease, and National Track and Field Hall of Famer

There are two primary reasons why the poor stay poor.

The first is a person's belief system. When I was young my immediate family was very poor, and so was my extended family. For most people in similar circumstances, the common belief is that being poor is just a way of life. If, for generations, everyone always has been poor, why should they think any differently for themselves? Our parents were poor, our grandparents were poor, our friends were poor, our neighbors were poor. Everyone we knew or associated with was poor. If no one within your environment has ever had money, why would your life be any different? My family, friends, and the community that surrounded us all believed that this was just the way it was and would always be. The idea that the future could be any better or different from what it always had been was considered foolish or arrogant. If no one within our family or community ever had much money, why would you be so arrogant to think that you could do better?

This negative belief system can be very debilitating. This lack of faith is one of the major challenges of why so many poor families continue to be poor.

Without a positive belief system of what is possible, it is extremely unlikely that the future will ever be bright. If we believe that our life cannot be any better, then why try? Instead, each day is about just getting by and doing the minimum, whether that be in school or work. We begin to accept whatever life brings our way. One of the most important lessons that I have learned in life is that life will give us whatever we are willing to accept. If attaining a better life is not possible, then why make the effort? After all, everything in life so far has been failure and disappointment. This mental hurtle is very real. It is both reinforced by psychological and social fears and it is a tremendous challenge to overcome. We all have fears and doubts and there is nothing more difficult to overcome. But the good news is they CAN be overcome. It is not easy, but it is a lot easier when you know where to begin.

If you come from a family or environment where wealth was rare or unheard of, and you are feeling doubtful, that is perfectly fine and, dare I say, normal. I struggled with these fears and doubts for many years and I understand the difficulty of overcoming it. This is why we (my daughter and I) are writing this book. Powering through fear and doubt, only to experience set back after set back, is very challenging. Over the course of my life, I have learned that there are only two ways to learn anything: one, from your experiences, and two, from someone else's. Which do you think is less painful? Learning from someone else is a much less painful approach, and it comes with fewer consequences. This book explains the journey of overcoming these psychological obstacles and the strategic financial challenges that we all face in trying to achieve financial security. When the goal of financial security is reached, the next goal for many is accumulating a comfortable level of wealth. We have outlined this book into chapters that you can reference long after you begin your investment journey, when you have questions about a particular aspect of accumulating wealth.

If you have enough faith and discipline to follow the plan, you will achieve financial security at a minimum and are more than likely to become wealthy. I have accomplished this in my own life through much trial and error and I've taught many others the formula that we will teach you here. You will be surprised at how simple it is once you understand the key principles to the process. I say it is simple --and it is! — but, like most things, it is simple when you know the right path and the pitfalls to avoid. This simple formula that we will teach you took me many, many years to figure out and it is my passion today to help others by sharing it.

If you're feeling doubtful, don't give up on yourself. We will help you establish the right belief system structure, provide healthy financial habits to stabilize your finances, and share with you the formula that will help you overcome these doubts and be successful.

Negativity disables us from accomplishing our dreams.

Negativity is like a disease. It feeds on hope, and skews our perspective. When one is surrounded by too much negativity, it becomes impossible to visualize success. Because one cannot believe they might be successful, they begin to think that failure is inevitable – even before they try. Negativity leads us to become debilitated by fear of failure and, instead of trying and failing, it is much easier to just accept one's fate and try to keep our expectations low. I know from personal experience that believing you cannot become financially secure is, for one thing, untrue, and for another thing, incredibly destructive to a person's actions. I will even take a bold step to say that the majority of Americans *do* have the capacity to become financially secure. But how do we achieve that first step and believe it is possible? One of my favorite scriptures illustrates the importance of faith:

According to your faith: Be it unto you. - Matthew 9:29.

To achieve anything, we need faith. Whatever you believe in is what will be. Throughout my lifetime I have found how true and powerful this verse is. Let me explain. We all will make a choice in life on what we believe in and what we attach our lives to. This choice may be conscious or subconscious. For example, some people in poverty believe that it is not possible to become wealthy. That belief clouds their judgment so that they cannot see opportunities to improve their circumstances. Therefore, they create a self-fulfilling prophecy: *I cannot become wealthy, therefore I will not.* No one accidentally woke up rich without believing it was possible and making an effort toward it. Those who focus on the value of material things fill their lives with clothes, new cars, and gadgets. Others who believe in faith and family invest time and attention to them and gain a greater sense of closeness because of their value system. For many people, the choice of what you believe in and ultimately gear your attention toward is almost automatic. This is why it is so important to think about what you value and what you are pursuing with a conscious mind and heart.

The reason this choice is so important, whether we know we have made the choice or not, is that it becomes the focus of our conscious and even subconscious. Whatever our minds are focused on, we will gravitate toward. Sometimes, this is a very conscious determined effort. At other times, it is our subconscious that takes over and, as if by gravity, we are steadily pulled in this direction. The pursuit of poverty generally is a subconscious decision that we make by giving up in the face of challenges. We accept what life is giving instead of refusing to accept this lot in life and seeking new opportunities to improve.

Where do you put your faith? It is possible to believe in more than just a religion. Whatever you value you begin to worship. What is the most important thing in the world to you? How do you visualize your life to be? Do you see yourself poor and struggling to keep a roof over the heads of your family? Do you see yourself in love with material things? Be thoughtful and careful what you wish for because you just might get it.

If you don't believe you can be successful then you are not going to accomplish much. If you don't try, then your lack of success is a self-fulfilling prophecy.

There are very few people raised in a lower income family that believe anything else is possible. That is the first thing that must change in order to change the gap between the rich and the poor. If you come from a lower income environment where negativity stifles anyone from trying to achieve anything, the first thing you have to do to become successful is change that belief system.

Standing on Your Own

A huge obstacle to overcoming negative belief systems is standing out from your friends and family in your pursuit to becoming successful. Very often, when a person of poverty goes against the grain, they are ridiculed for it. Other members in the community will ridicule that person and ask them: Why do you think you're better than everyone else? This creates a social gap between the person trying to work hard and the other that has accepted having the bare minimum job, minimum wage, and minimum expectations. These psychological hurtles and environmental factors can become permanent and impossible to overcome. The social obstructions and psychological component of your belief system are both very important. They will determine your success simply by driving your ability to act and work. If you feel insecure and believe you're going to fail, you risk making actions from a place of fear, becoming inactive, and eventually giving up. If you believe it is possible, you will find and secure opportunities to change your circumstances and you will make a difference. It is your decision to pursue the life of your dreams. If you are confronted by others or put down by them, stay humble and let it go. Do not let others define who you are. You must define who you are by taking the right steps to the future you desire. Welcome others to come with you, but if they choose not to, then accept their choice and move on.

Environmental Negativity

I have personally felt the crushing weight of negative thinking even after I had attained some success in the real estate industry.

Early in my career, I tried to surround myself with successful people to learn more from them. But when I did, I often felt inadequate or even fake. I felt like I was faking my ability to be successful and I frequently had moments of great doubt in myself. I thought, "Why should I be in this group of successful people that are well educated? What makes me believe that I deserve to be here, where I know no one?" I felt no sense of belonging. There was a great deal of insecurity I had to overcome when I began to compete in that environment. It was also difficult to feel belonging because I came from a family where no one had achieved any significant level of financial success. I know how powerful the sense of fear can be. It is as if gravity is pulling you toward your comfort zone, telling you to retreat to what feels safe and natural. But know that being uncomfortable in this context is good. It means that you are pushing your boundaries and spreading your opportunities for growth, so long as you listen and look for them. It feels much safer to just stay in your comfort zone, even if it means being poor, simply because you feel you belong there. If you want to become wealthy, you need to learn to resist that comfort and continue to push through. Get comfortable with feeling uncomfortable.

As a loan officer, I gave presentations all over Southern California. Early in my career, when I went to poorer communities such as Inglewood or Southgate, I felt very comfortable presenting to lower income groups because that was the community I came from. If I gave presentations to wealthy, educated people in Orange County, I would get so nervous I could barely deliver them. I would sweat bullets and I thought, "These people are so much smarter than me. Why am I doing this? Why am I speaking to them?"

Getting out of that mindset was not easy for me, psychologically or emotionally, but I can promise that it ends, and the rewards for breaking through are multiple and great.

Knowing the Way

The rich have two big advantages over the poor in achieving success. The first is the psychological component. This is such a crucial factor of your success. In most cases, the psychological challenge of believing that it is possible to become rich is limited to the poor. If you are born rich you expect to always be rich. The question *Can I be rich?* does not exist, because you already have wealth. Imagine the difference of starting any competition knowing you have won that competition in the past and most everyone you know has won in the past? The fear or doubt is almost completely absent, the question isn't *if* you are going to be successful, the question is *how* successful you will be.

The second advantage is their access to information and knowledge through their family and network of friends. The most important of these advantages begins with a parent. Having access on a daily basis to a one-on-one mentor, who has been taught, through both formal education and life lessons, how to be successful in the pursuit of a career and/or financial investments, is invaluable. A wealthy parent has an investment portfolio with which they have consulted with top financial planners for years. Another advantage is having a parent who knows the best educational path through public or private schools that will provide the best preparation for whatever career direction the child may choose. This access to a personal mentor is a tremendous advantage over those who do not have a mentor. Families that have found success go to great lengths to protect the wealth they have created and preserve it through a legacy plan. Assets are wisely invested as a result of strategic planning with the best investment minds they could hire. The other major advantage is their network of affluent people.

Whether you want to accumulate wealth or accomplish a specific goal, you need to figure out how to do so. If you don't know how to do it yourself, you must learn from someone. If you come from a wealthy family, there are people within close reach, whether it be family, friends or through hiring talented professionals to provide the knowledge in financial or business matters. This access to information makes it so much easier to learn the formulas that work and warn you of the pitfalls to avoid. The educational advantage the rich have is access to superior schools and colleges. As I said before, generally speaking, there is minimal financial education in our school system unless you pursue a specific degree in finance. Wealthy families that establish financial security typically instill the lessons they've learned in their children, who then have access to the resources to maintain that wealth. They have access to the same financial advisors who don't advise the less fortunate because they do not have a large enough asset base for a financial advisor to invest and make money from. Many financial advisors have a minimum $250,000 in investable assets before they will spend any time consulting a possible client. Compare this to middle and lower income folks who not only don't have the know-how, but also don't have access to the people with the skills and knowledge in financial literacy. Wealthy people not only have their family, they also have a network of people to turn to as a resource. This advantage of access to information is absolutely huge in achieving success. It is my hope that this book and our Mark 1 Wealth Academy web site will be helpful tools to provide you some of the information you will need.

Two of the biggest problems that affect the gap between the rich and the poor are: 1) the infrastructure of environmental negativity in low socio-economic neighborhoods and 2) the complexity of belief systems. That is why I wanted to write this book -- to help you overcome the psychological factors and learn the step-by-step process of how to accumulate wealth as safely and reliably as possible. I'll also discuss how to convert that wealth to cash flow for retirement so you will have the income that you need. Changing your circumstances *is possible* and I want to show you how.

Can a man change his stars?

One of my favorite movies is about a young poor boy who dreams of becoming a knight. The poor boy hears a man laugh at his expense and the boy asks his father, "Can a man change his stars?" *Stars*, of course, refers to his fate. The father answers, "Yes, William. If he believes enough, a man can do anything." You may recognize this film by its title, *A Knight's Tale*. One of the excellent themes of that movie is the idea that a person can change his or her destiny through belief, hard work and determination. It's a very American trope, but a true one at that. I am a strong believer in this because once upon a time, I was a young, poor boy dreaming of a better life.

My Financial Journey

If you've ever turned on a radio and flipped through the channels, you've probably heard rappers singing about gang life in my hometown. I grew up in the poor part of South Los Angeles in the infamous city of Compton. Both my parents were uneducated. Neither of them even had a high school diploma. My mother was born to immigrant parents of Mexican and Italian descent, and my father dropped out of seventh grade in North Carolina to hitchhike to LA when he was only fourteen. Growing up, I moved constantly from school to school as my father worked from job to job at steel mills and other low-paying jobs while my mother worked in various retail stores. My extended families on both sides were uneducated. Everyone around me, from my family to my friends to the kids I went to school with, was poor. No one around me believed in even *trying* to become wealthy. Their main financial concern was to *not* be poor. Getting by was the only goal.

This mindset is a common one in low-income communities and it is an essential part of why the poor struggle to improve their circumstances. I will expound on this mindset, and how to overcome it, later on in an in-depth chapter. The important thing to realize is that the mindset of just doing enough to get by will ruin your chances even before you try to become wealthy. The main reason the community I grew up in did not have high financial goals was because no one believed that it was even *possible* to change their circumstances.

The best thing my parents said to me was that the opportunity for more existed in this country. They always told me that in America it was possible to achieve more. They founded a belief system that taught me to believe that good things could happen and you can change your circumstances. From this belief system I was able to envision my dreams and had the encouragement to try to fulfill them. So, despite being surrounded by people trod upon with grief and unhappiness, I was not limited by the negativity and dejectedness. Even though I believed that there could be more, I did not know how to make that happen -- but I was willing to try and make the effort.

When I graduated high school I enrolled in a few business classes at the local junior college, Cypress College, and spent one semester there. My only goal was to make money now. I did not want to wait four or five years in college, which I would have been paying for myself. I knew at eighteen years old that I could get a real estate license and have a real job. Real estate was of interest to me because I could begin immediately and because it was an industry where the opportunities to make money were great.

In the 70s, the economy was booming, inflation was on the rise. People were buying and property values were going up. The market was improving rapidly and I was finally starting to make money and save when, in 1980, it all came to a halt. The Federal Reserve Chairman, Paul Volker, started raising interest rates to slow down inflation and choke off money supply. The real estate and mortgage industry came to a stop and I learned my first big financial lesson. My income took a drastic drop and I had to live off my savings for a while until business started turning up. The good news was, as painful as that was, I was only 22 years old and I learned at a young age about recessions. This essential lesson was crucial to the future of my business because I learned how to withstand highs and lows in the real estate and mortgage industry. Throughout my life there have been many ups and downs in the economy. My company survived the housing bubble of 2008 when all of my competitors were drowning and closing out. I learned to adapt, but it was not easy and it was painful. Now, I want to share my knowledge of real estate investments with you so that you can also have a successful income that will help you grow wealthy, save for retirement, and improve your circumstances.

The Road is Long

Over the years there have been many bumps in the road and with each bump I've learned what works and what doesn't work. The point of this book is to teach you where the potholes in the road are so you don't have as many bumps. Anyone can follow my path in investing, but without the formula and guidance, how can they know where to begin? I am writing this book to share my financial knowledge with others so that those in the middle and lower income groups can also have access to gaining financial security and wealth and overcoming poverty.

You might be thinking, "Oh, brother, he is spewing pipe dreams to sell books!" But I assure you, this is not the case. In fact, all profits from the sale of this book are being donated to charity. If you will invest the time into reading this book, you will learn a step-by-step process that will guide you to becoming wealthy through a gradual method with very low risk. The purpose of this book is to teach and inspire you to not only reach a life of financial security but to become wealthy! For those that come from similar origins as me, I want to get to the crux of the issue why many Americans will never be wealthy—because they don't *believe* they can be.

The Power of Positive Thinking

"Most folks are about as happy as they make up their minds to be."

– Abraham Lincoln

A person can have all of the tools for success, such as a supportive family, access to education and a job opportunity, but still never overcome adversity because they lack the most crucial and fundamental element: belief in himself. If you are ever to accomplish anything, you must have a determined belief in yourself. This can be a very hard thing to find for some people. Perhaps they've had poor relationships with their family, which have led to emotional and sometimes physical abuse, making it very hard for them to think positively about themselves. One thing I've learned about successful people is that each one has the belief that, yes, they can do it.

Chapter Two

Why Americans Need Money More Than Ever Before

46% of American workers
have less than 10,000 in
savings
29% have less than $1,000
25% have 0

-Reported by the Employee Benefits Research
Institute in 2007

The Rich Get Richer and the Poor Get Poorer

The gap between the rich and the poor in America has never been wider nor has it grown faster than over the past 30 years.

Why do so many have so little?

There are two reasons.

1. Americans struggle to save money.

2. Many are not financially literate in wealth building strategies.

How did this gap widen so quickly, road blocking so many American families from supporting their children? The problem is wages and inflation. Wages do not increase fast enough to outpace inflation, and the cost of living steadily grows. The rich have assets and benefit from inflation, while the poor do not have assets and fall behind, thus the rich get richer and the poor get poorer. Most people do not know how to increase their net income and will never become rich. But let's talk about the real danger that lurks in the future -- financial security and retirement.

Unfortunate (and Scary) Facts about American Workers Today:

Most Americans will never be able to retire. In the last 20 years, the number of companies that have private pension plans for employees have plummeted. Today, according to Money Magazine, 13% of private companies offer pensions for their employees. Thirty years ago private company pension plans began to disappear and the 401K was created to provide a substitute. Unfortunately for many, most of today's jobs with pension plans are reserved for governmental positions so unless you want to become a police officer or firefighter you will need to find a better retirement plan.

Currently, 70% of Americans are unable to retire long term and the number is rapidly increasing. The simple fact is that most people cannot save their way to financial security and retirement because it is mathematically impossible.

To quote *Real Estate Investing* by Gary W. Eldred,

"Most Americans can't afford to retire. Social Security has become the only remaining financial crutch for retirement."

But what about my 401k or IRA?

If you currently work for a company that provides a 401 k plan or if you've set up your own IRA you may be thinking that you're doing your part in establishing a secure retirement plan. In today's economy a 401 k is important. However, the **key reason the 401k /IRS is failing the average person is inflation.** The constant rising cost of goods and services exceed many people's ability to save. Sadly, very few people recognize this before it is too late. Most live their lives saving what they can until they reach their senior years and learn the painful lesson that the slow growth of their 401k/IRS is not enough to compensate for the rapid growth of inflation has crushed their hopes of retiring. To make matter worse, the actual inflation rate for Southern California consumers is much higher. The reason is the cost of housing. Rents in Southern California have been going up approximately 5% per year. Home ownership has been even higher. Sales prices in Los Angeles and Orange Counties have been rising over an average of 8.5% during this same period. Thus, putting Southern California families in even more danger of not being able to retire. **But don't worry. We'll go over the simple path to using inflation to your benefit.**

How could good, hard-working Americans fall into this pit? The reason is because of the lack of company pension plans, poor spending habits, and lack of knowledge on how to increase their income. Seventy percent of Americans will never be able to retire because they don't know how to accumulate the necessary wealth. That means two-thirds of Americans will work their entire lives. How could this happen? There are many reasons, but the primary reasons are the global economy and technology. American companies are now fighting to compete with global powers like China, where wages are far lower than they are in the U.S. In addition, millions of manufacturing jobs have gone to Mexico and hundreds of thousands of service and administration jobs have gone to

India. Today's technology allows an employee to sit literally anywhere on the planet while working. These factors make it impossible for U.S. companies to compete with U.S. wages so they are moving jobs all over the planet. This downward pressure on wages has also hurt retirement programs for employees. Even though this restructuring has pulled the rug from so many workers who will likely not be able to save enough money in time to retire, there is a path to financial security -- so don't lose hope.

Millions of Americans are unprepared for retirement for one simple piece of information they don't have: **Most Americans do not know how much money they need to save to create the investment income they will need to retire**. Since they don't know, they are not saving enough and will likely fall into that 65%. I am trying to bring awareness to the retirement crisis in America and offering a plausible solution for any person, from the modest in wages to the most affluent. I hope by discussing this issue and explaining every step to my formula for success we will hopefully begin to turn the tide on the 65%.

To resolve your retirement issues, you need to answer:

1. **How much income will I need at the time of retirement?**

2. **How much will I need to save to provide the income I need?**

3. **How will I accumulate this money?**

Let's tackle each of these questions.

Question 1: How much income will you need at the time of your retirement?

Let's get started by analyzing your current budget. Prepare a list including your rent or mortgage payment, car payment, insurance, food, entertainment, etc. Let's say these expenses total $3,000 per month and that you are 30 years old and that you want to retire at age 60. How much will inflation increase these same expenses in 30 years?

Now let's look at one of your highest necessary payments: housing. As a general rule, most people's housing expense is approximately 45-50% of their expenses. If you rent, how much will your rent increase on an annual basis in your community? In Southern California, rents have averaged annual increases of 3-4%, depending on location. So let's calculate what your total living expenses will be in 30 years.

Compound Interest Calculator

Use this calculator to determine how much your money can grow using the power of compound interest.

Current Principal: $3,000
Years to Grow: 30
Interest Rate: 3%

Results

Future Value $7,281

Data Source: Investor.gov

Using a 3% inflation rate, your expenses will increase to $7,281 per month!

As you can see, your total monthly expenses almost triple! My suggestion in planning for retirement is to make two calculations. Using a compounding calculator from the web, calculate your monthly future expenses using an inflation rate of 2% and at 3% to determine what your future expenses will be at the time of your retirement. This way you will have a strong idea and a range of what your expenses will be at the time of retirement.

Assuming your total current expenses are $3,000 per month and your retirement date is 30 years off, you would need to have a net monthly income of $7,281. So if you need $7,281 per month in net income to pay your bills each month when you retire, then you would need a monthly income of approximately $10,000 per month in gross income and an annual income of $120,000.

Are you getting the idea of why so many are unable to retire?

Question 2- How much money will you need to save to provide the income you need?

It depends on what your rate of return is on the money you have saved or invested. Each person's threshold for risk varies. Generally speaking, people will assume more risk when they are young and become more conservative as they get older because as they age they no longer have the time to make up for losses. Start reviewing the types of returns that you have been earning on the existing investments, which you may have in an IRA or other retirement vehicle.

As you probably know, stashing your money in the bank is not going to pay you a very high return so let's assume your investment is elsewhere and you are receiving a 6% rate of return. If we use the scenario above, that requires we have $120,000 per year income, this means that if we divide this amount by a 6% rate of return it equals $2,000,000 in savings or assets over the 30 years that we will need to have to retire.

Is that what you expected? Probably not. Most people are shocked to see how fast the numbers multiply. The number one mistake people make is underestimating what their future expenses will be. They fail to incorporate inflation into their calculation and this unfortunately leaves millions of people unprepared for retirement, even if they've been saving their whole lives, either because they haven't done any calculations or their calculations are far too low.

Let's use a compound calculator to estimate how much money you would accumulate at various savings rates. Let's say you save $200 per month for a total of $2,400 per year and receive a 7% rate of return.

Compound Interest Calculator

Use this calculator to determine how much your money can grow using the power of compound interest.

Current Principal: $2,400	
Monthly Addition: $200	
Years to Grow: 30	
Interest Rate: 7%	

Results

Future Value $245,617

Data Source: Investor.gov

$245,617 is a pretty good sum, however, this savings will only provide $1,429 per month in income, not nearly the monthly income that you will need to be retire and be financially secure.

Okay. Let's say you bulk up more than that in savings and in income. Let's say you save $10,000 to put into a savings investment and you add $500 a month for 30 years at a 6% interest rate. You'd hope all the hard work of saving $10,000 and the $500 addition per month would gain some ground after 30 years.

Compound Interest Calculator

Use this calculator to determine how much your money can grow using the power of compound interest.

Top of Form

Current Principal: $ 10,000
Monthly Addition: $ 500
Years to Grow: 30
Interest Rate: 8%

Results

Future Value $780,325.84

Data Source: Investor.gov

As you can see, its better but you're still going to fall woefully short of $2,000,000. It is also exceptionally difficult to secure an 8% interest rate or rate of return year in and year out.

I hope you are beginning to understand why it is so difficult for people in the middle and lower income groups to achieve financial security and ultimately be able to retire. The good news is there is a solution and a path to follow and not just for the rich but for the average working person.

The Importance of Saving

The first big mistake that most people make is they simply don't save their money. Saving your money is not complicated, but it does take discipline and a system, a system we call a budget. You MUST sit down and analyze a balance of your lifestyle and savings rate. It is easy to spend all of your money regardless of how much you make. There is always a bigger, nicer place to live or car to drive. We must make financial security our number priority, not impressing our friends and neighbors.

Millions of people do not realize how much money they will need to stabilize an income when they want to retire. Because they have no idea, it is easy to get in the habit of ignoring it. Some people assume that with pay raises they will be able to save enough in time, but they don't factor in inflation, which is as inescapable as death and taxes. If you don't figure this out now, and don't formulate a plan, you are going to be part of the 65% (which is likely to grow) that will work until the day they die.

What about the government?

The issue of retirement and our social security system is just one more on the long list of issues fighting to get addressed in Washington D.C. However, Congress isn't working on increasing your social security income. Instead, Washington is working on keeping social security financially viable by increasing the age in which you can begin collecting. The government is not a reliable solution.

Since 1984, the net worth gap between the wealthy and the middle incomes has grown from 3.5 to more than 7 times. The gap between the rich and the poor is now 700 times wider. How is this possible? The Obama administration is one of the most progressive administrations that the U.S. has seen in generations. This administration was supposed to be more focused on improving conditions for the poor and middle class than any before, but instead the gap between the rich and poor has only widened at an accelerating pace. I am not a political or economical theorist nor will I pretend to be. However, there is one thing that is clear. For over thirty years, through both Republican and Democratic administrations, the gap between the rich and poor has gotten wider. The government is not the solution for Americans. There are no quick-fix solutions to improving the gap between the wealthy and the poor. But I can offer you a solution that will protect your family and significantly increase your net worth for the rest of your life.

Regardless of all the battles politicians get into and the debates they hold on television, we cannot rely on them to solve the problem. We, as a people, have to solve our own problems. This means that you are on your own more than ever! Company pension plans have either been discontinued or gutted by virtually every industry with the exception of government workers, both state and federal.

What about schools? Did we miss out on financial education in high school or college by not paying attention? Or was it never really there?

Financial Education in Schools

A debilitating factor that disempowers poor communities is the lack of financial education in our schools. Public or private, high school or college, American schools provide little to no educational programs, even on the most elementary budgeting skills. There are no required classes on managing finances, even in college, and because of this, there is little infrastructure to help young students learn how to earn a steady income and be able to afford a comfortable lifestyle. How can we teach young men and women to have big dreams of buying a house and starting a family but then send them into the world lacking such an important life skill?

The most skilled and trained financial planners and investment bankers have little interest in spending time educating middle- and lower-income people simply because there is no incentive to do so. If there's one thing they know, it's the value of using time wisely — to make money. There usually is a high cost for valuable information; however, this book offers my financial guidance and will teach you how to attain financial security.

Real Estate Investing: The Key to a Life of Financial Stability

When I tell most people that they can turn a $25,000 investment into a one-million-dollar profit, I get two different reactions: the first is disbelief, as if I am telling them a cruel joke. The second is great cynicism and, if they don't know me, a feeling of distrust as if I am trying to sell them a beachfront property in Utah. If this is true, they think, then why isn't everyone doing it? Most middle to lower income people do not know the formula for becoming wealthy, not because it doesn't exist, but because of the way valuable information is passed down from wealthy person to wealthy person. Mid to lower income people do not learn wise practices because they do have not an example to learn from and because so many schools do not teach the tools to become wealthy. Some people assume I'm a salesperson trying to make a quick buck by selling some get-rich-quick scheme. This isn't true either. Real estate investing is one of the safest, consistently high-yielding investments available to the average person. The proof is in the numbers.

An Overview of the Plan

When we are young, very often we dream of becoming rich and being able to buy anything we want. But for most of us, as the years go by, we learn just how hard it is to provide for a family and build wealth. In time, our objective changes to: "I just want to have a secure financial life."

Accumulating the money needed to achieve the financial security you want for your family takes a great deal of hard work, discipline, and of course, a plan. I can't promise you the hard work or the discipline, you have to bring that yourself, but I can certainly help you with the plan.

Having a plan is probably the most important aspect of achieving wealth. Consider this plan your roadmap. When you are traveling, can you imagine trying to reach your destination without a roadmap or in today's age, Google Maps? Of course not, and that's why my roadmap to wealth can be a valuable tool for you to use to accomplish your wealth-building goals. In the following pages, I am going to explain a few of the basics about real estate investing. While your initial house purchase may seem to be just something you buy where your family will live, it's actually your first real estate investment and your first step on your road to financial security. Knowing how to use this investment correctly in building wealth is the key! Not only do few homeowners know how to do this, very few Realtors know how to do this. The reason? They aren't trained. Realtors who sell residential real estate are trained how to list and sell properties. They are NOT trained how to strategically invest in real estate.

As a result, the blind lead the blind when it comes to real estate as an investment. This is why so many people miss out on this incredible path to financial security and wealth. When it comes to investing and retirement, very often people rely on a financial planner to prepare their retirement plan. While there are many highly skilled and trained financial planners, most focus on what they sell:

stocks, bonds, annuities, and other insurance products. Real estate is usually not something they are familiar with and they tend to think of real estate as a way to own a home, not an investment that will gain you wealth.

My formula illustrates an alternative path that can enable you to grow your assets faster, with greater reliability than any other type of investment.

Good Investing Means Financial Independence

Financial independence means the accumulation of enough income-generating assets to enable you to comfortably live off those assets without needing to continue working. Having discipline to save money is the first step, but without a good investment plan it will likely fall short of getting you where you want to go. Because families require not only housing, but also big-ticket items such as cars, college, and vacations, it's certainly difficult to save for the near future -- let alone for your retirement years. Taking this into account, my Roadmap to Wealth can guide you, step-by-step, helping you ultimately reach your financial goals.

Limited Financial Advice Can Cost You Thousands

As I stated earlier, when a person goes to a financial advisor asking for help to plan for retirement and invest their savings, these advisors often present only financial products such as securities (stocks, bonds, and mutual funds) and insurance products such as annuities. I believe it is critical to have a diversified investment portfolio, so I would never suggest my clients (or friends) have only real estate in their portfolios. However, I am insistent that real estate must be a part of that diversification in order for my clients to receive maximum return and security of their investments.

Surprisingly, most people are unaware of just how superior the rate of return is on real estate compared to these other investments. The Mark 1 Wealth Academy ROI (Return on Investment) forecaster can assist you in doing projections that illustrate how you can reach your financial goals.

Three Keys to Real Estate Investment

While I can show examples of how and why real estate is a wise investment strategy, first let's break it down to the simple facts of investing and why they work so well in real estate. Real estate outperforms other investments because of these powerful rules of investments:

1. Compounding

2. Leverage

3. Time (staying the course)

Let's define these terms.

Compounding

The power of compounding manifests when your investment is multiplied by earning additional dollars on top of the previous dividends paid. Compounding makes more people wealthy faster than any other strategy. There are two important factors to compounding:

- **Rate of return** - The higher your rate of return, the faster your money will grow.
- **Time** - Over time, your investment will multiply—so the sooner you get started, the sooner your dividends increase.

The Importance of Time in Compounding

This chart illustrates that the earlier you invest, the faster your wealth accumulates. A person starting at age 34 will have to invest for 30 years to reach approximately the same point as a person who started 10 years earlier and only invested for 10 years.

The Power of Leverage

Nearly every investment has the compounding effect. But few investments have the power of leverage. Leverage is when you obtain a loan to provide the funds to invest. To do this with stocks is extremely risky. If the company you invest in fails, or the stock market experiences an extreme drop, the lender will most likely "call the loan." When this happens, your investment in the stock market may completely dissolve. This is not the case with a mortgage on real estate. While a foreclosure could signal the loss of your real estate investment, with prudent real estate investment decisions, this is unlikely.

The tremendous advantage that leverage creates for real estate investments is that your rate of return is not based on your investment or on the down payment. Instead, it is based on the value of the property. This is called leverage and it's what protects most real estate investments. Here is one comparison of your investment in real estate versus investing in the stock market.

Why Time (Staying the Course) is Essential to Earning Your Returns

Staying the course means letting time work the magic of compounding your return. This is a critical part of achieving financial independence and stability. Your Roadmap to Wealth Plan requires you to have the discipline to stay the course for it to be successful.

Two big mistakes that could ruin your investment:

- **Careless spending:** Many consumers' savings strategies are derailed by shopping habits that are driven by ego gratification. While everyone enjoys the finer things in life, a person on the road to wealth can make a huge mistake by focusing on expensive clothing, designer furniture, exotic perfumes, and luxury cars. There are many decisions that you will make that have nothing to do with investing that could cripple your ability to be financially secure and ultimately wealthy. The **majority** of Americans are puppets to status. They spend too much of their money on cars, clothes, shoes, purses, and toys of all kinds just to keep up with the Jones's as they say. This daily temptation and your ability to control and manage these temptations will determine whether you are able to save money to invest or not. If you do not learn to control your spending and continually spend excessively on status items, you will become a slave to status and your ego.

• **Cashing in early:** The biggest mistake made by the typical consumer is selling their first home purchase. Some consumers start off right by investing in real estate. They buy their first house and then, five to seven years later, they sell the house and buy a larger property with a larger mortgage. While they have a larger house to live in, two unfortunate things happen with this strategy. First, they make the mistake of trading in early. For example, say a homebuyer sold their first home for $300,000 and moved up and purchased a new bigger home for $400,000. If instead they kept the first property worth $300,000 and then rented it and purchased a new home for $300,000 they would now have two properties with a total asset value of $600,000. The compounding on assets of $600,000 is going to grow far higher than on a single asset of $400,000.

Secondly, by buying a larger home the consumer has a larger mortgage and no help in making the payment that a renter would provide had they kept the first property. This now larger mortgage debt brings with it a larger mortgage payment, a higher property tax bill, higher utilities and more upkeep costs. Additionally, by not having a rental property there will not be any rental income growing each year as inflation allows you to increase rents are create retirement income. Selling your first home purchase is a HUGE mistake! As a result this person's real estate investment plan has gone nowhere.

These are some of the most common mistakes potential investors make. I will delve further into the roadblocks and hurdles as you go on your journey in later chapters.

If you wonder why staying the course is so important, consider that price appreciation in California has grown consistently since 1968. While there are peaks and valleys, the California Association of Realtors reports that California real estate has increased by over 7.3% annually during this time period. Nationally it's a little lower, about 5% per year. With this information, you can see why it pays for you to begin watching that growth continue, thereby enabling you to live a financially secure life.

My objective is to help you develop and execute a long-term investment plan to achieve your financial goals. I help my clients successfully create and manage their real estate portfolio in order for them to increase:

- **Balance**
- **Safety**
- **Rate of Return**
- **Tax deductions**

Let me explain why each of this is so important.

Balance

The ideal balanced investment portfolio includes stocks, bonds, and real estate. This enables you to diversify, and thereby strengthen, your financial position. If one starts to do poorly you have the other to balance it out.

Safety

I am fully aware of the risks of real estate investing and my top priority is to ensure that my clients make educated, informed real estate investments. I collaborate with my clients to ensure that strategic, cautious decisions are made that mitigate risks as much as possible, and I will do the same with you in the following chapters. Some key areas that affect the safety of real estate investment are: location, property condition, and legal compliance with the city, county, and state regulations, to name a few.

Rate of Return

We all want the best rate of return on our investments – with as little risk as possible. Securing a favorable rate of return, with a comfortable level of risk, is the objective. Potential investments range from the most conservative FDIC-insured bank account to the often-volatile stock market to real estate.

Why is real estate the best choice? Very simply, when compared with the rest, it can provide an excellent rate of return with the least amount of risk. Viewed over the past 25 years, the return on investment through real estate has been far superior to stock market investments. Investing in stocks can be risky because even large companies can go under during financial crises. And while property values do decline during recessions, if real estate investors have bought carefully and not become overly leveraged, the property is still standing when the economy picks up and values begin to climb again. A further advantage occurs for investors who have rental property, as rents usually rise during a financial crisis, creating security for retired investors counting on this income. Overall, the demand for Southern California real estate today is stronger than ever, and the demand is even global.

Tax Deductions

Real estate investments have many tax advantages over other investments and we can provide guidance as you consider purchases that are right for you. However, it's important to consult with a Certified Public Accountant for specifics on the tax benefits of the particular type of real estate you are considering. I have also consulted with a variety of legal experts and asked them to contribute valuable educational information for my clients and for you. Check out my Wealth Academy blog for expert videos and blog posts on how to invest wisely and protect your assets.

www.mark1wealthacademy.com

Chapter Three

Why Real Estate is the Fastest and Safest Path to Wealth

We all want to know what is the fastest **AND** safest path to wealth! This topic has been debated I am sure for centuries and everyone has an opinion but the fact is real estate is absolutely, positively the fastest and safest path to wealth and it is essential you know and understand why.

Now fast without safe is of no real value long term and hopefully your financial life is something you view as long term.

In this chapter I am going to demonstrate to you **why** real estate is the fastest and safest path to wealth.

The Secret Sauce to Real Estate! The Utility Value

Have you ever watched the TV show Shark Tank?
On the show you will see an entrepreneur pitch their business model or idea to the Sharks/ Investors. Very often you will then hear Mark Cuban or one of the Sharks ask, "What is the secret sauce to your business?" here's what he's really asking. "What is the insurmountable competitive advantage that your business has?"

A patent would be a good example of an insurmountable competitive advantage for a business.

Real Estate has an insurmountable advantage over every other asset class that very few people are aware of and because of this never discuss. Real estate's insurmountable competitive edge over every other investment is it's utility value. When you purchase real estate or property that has a structure on it whether it be residential or commercial this structure has the ability to be used. This usage very often has a value, the amount will vary depending on if it is a residential property for rent, commercial, or warehouse etc.

Now let's compare this to investing in stocks.

The Utility Value of Real Estate

ASSUMPTIONS	Stock RENT	Real Estate RESIDENCE	Real Estate RENTAL
Initial Investment Amount	$120,000	$120,000	$120,000
Initial Investment Value	$120,000	$600,000	$600,000
Growth Rate	8%	5%	5%
Monthly Housing Expense	($3,000)	($3,279)	($3,279)
Monthly Housing Income	$0	$0	$3,000
Annual Rent Increase	4%	NA	4%
RESULTS			
Investment Value 30 Years	$1,207,519	$2,593,165	$2,593,165
Total 30 Year Housing Expense	($2,019,058)	($1,180,407)	($1,126,406)
Total 30 Year Housing Income	$0	$0	$2,019,058
Total 30 Year Maintenance/Operating Expense	$0	($90,000)	($403,812)
Total 30 Year Value	($811,539)	$1,322,758	$3,082,005

Let's start on the top left with investing $120,000 in the stock market in return for your investment you will receive $120,000 in stock certificates. What can you use these stock certificates for? Answer, maybe wallpaper!

We will start with analyzing a stock investment and its return on investment. Because stocks do not have the utility value or the ability for you to live in the stock certificates this means you must pay for a place to live or be homeless. The utility value of real estate is an insurmountable competitive advantage in creating income and wealth growth. Lets examine exactly how much this utility value difference is worth on a typical residential home investment versus investing in stocks and renting.

Let's say the stock investor is earning a healthy 8% net return on their stocks, now for you to earn 8% net after management fees means that your gross earnings have to be close to 10% annually which is extremely unlikely over a 30-year period.

My point is, I'm slanting the deck in favor of the stock market and against Real Estate.

Monthly housing expense. Let's say you're renting for $3,000 a month. California rents, on average have appreciated 4.7% for the past 50 years. I'm only using 4%.

In 30 years, your stock portfolio is worth $1.2 million. A financial planner or a stock broker would be very proud of getting you 8% net return over 30 years, or $1.2 million. But because the stocks have no utility means you would have had to pay over $2 million in rent leaving a financial loss of over $800,000 over that same period, meaning the renter actually went backwards financially and didn't know it.

Now let's take that same $120,000 as a 20% down payment on a $600,000 property, we will only use an appreciation rate of 5% not the 50 years California historical average of 7.3%. You can see the mortgage payment which includes principal, interest, taxes, and insurance. In 30 years, you have an asset worth two-and-a-half-million dollars. You would have paid 1.1 million for that asset. Next is money allocated for maintenance expenses like carpet and paint. Your net profit is over $1.3 million.
Here's the point, the utility value of real estate due to the ability to use the land and the structure versus stocks that have no utility is worth over $ two million dollars to you.

Do you know how many renters know or consider this when renting? Absolutely none... They don't know.
Do you know how many realtors know this? Maybe 1%, now let's go to the third column with a rental property. Let's say a homeowner turns their home into a rental, using the same financial numbers in 30 years they have a two-and-a-half-million-dollar asset that has collected $3,000 a month over 30 years, the total is over 2 million dollars for the utility. The total gain is over $3 million for the real estate versus $1.2 million on stocks.

Because of this insurmountable advantage that real estate has over other assets real estate will on average real estate **triple** the wealth growth over stocks.

Given these facts about the wealth growth of real estate it is more amazing to learn how few own investments in real estate. I want to share with you some startling statistics.

In Los Angeles County only about 7% of the people own two or more properties, in Orange County it's about 10%, but guess what percent have a 401k's or IRA? 32% have a 401K and 33% have a IRA, some people have both due to job changes but when you average it out approximately 40-50% of the working population have one of these retirement accounts but no investment real estate. How is it possible that the stock market via the 401K or IRA has a market share of 4-5 times GREATER than real estate?

The obvious answer is a lack of knowledge or financial literacy. The residential real estate industry of sales agents are not trained on the financial dynamics of real estate wealth growth! They are trained in two areas, 1- on how to be salespeople, meaning how to market and prospect for clients. 2- how to sell residential real estate as if they were selling a commodity like an appliance.

WHY Real Estate is the fastest and safest way to build wealth!

There are two reasons why real estate is the fastest way to build wealth:

1- Is the utility value that we have already discussed.
2- The five economic benefits of real estate, what this means is that you the property owner are making money five different ways. There is no other asset that can say this!

Let's review these five different ways:

1- Appreciation- appreciation is the one economic benefit that everyone is aware of, appreciation is the percentage of the properties increased value. Because many people think appreciation is the only economic benefit, they believe that stocks outperform real estate in wealth growth when in reality real estate in most parts of the country will consistently outperform stocks and it's not even close.

2- Principal Reduction- In most cases borrowers secure a mortgage that is fully amortized over 30 or 15 years. On a 30 year fully amortized loan at an interest rate of 4% approximately 58% of the mortgage payment is principal reduction. (As interest rates rise the percentage of principal goes down.) What this means is when a tenant makes a rent payment and you in turn use this money to make the mortgage payment the principal on the loan is paid down creating equity in the property which is the equivalent of money in the bank. Because of the utility value of real estate, real estate is the only asset that you can leverage and get **someone else** to pay off the leverage. If you were going to leverage your stocks which is extremely risky to begin with, who would pay off your leverage? Answer- no one, because there is no utility to stocks.

3- Rental Cash Flow- rents basically go one way, they go up. It is extremely rare for a property owner to call a tenant and say, "I have good news, I have decided to reduce your rent!" Have you ever received that call?

4- Tax benefits- real estate has the incredible phantom paper loss of depreciation. Depreciation is the tax deduction allowed by the IRS to expense the building for wear and tear (not the land) of the structure. Residential real estate is depreciated for 27.5 years, commercial is 39 years. What this means is that the value of the structure is divided by the IRS allowable depreciable years to arrive at an annual amount that can be deducted from your income on the property. Over the years this amount can be quite sizable. The most recent tax reform act of 2017 has added an additional tax benefit of 20% tax free income on real estate investments and services. (See your CPA for details on this.)

5- Leverage- what this means is that you are making money not only on your money, which is the down payment (assuming you made one keep in mind you can often times buy real estate with no money down) and the banks money or the mortgage that you got when you purchased the property.

Now let's review what this means in dollars and cents to you the homeowner or investor. Let's say you invest $65,000 into the stock market which then gets you $65,000 worth of stock. But you could use this same $65,000 and put a 10% down payment to purchase a $650,000 property. You now have an asset 10x the size of a stock investment with the same amount of money.

See the slide below comparing a 5% return on your stock account versus only 4% on real estate. As you can see it is not close in annual return on investment.

The Five Economic Benefits of Real Estate

		Retirement Account	Real Estate	
	Investment Amount	$65,000	$65,000	Your $'s are multiplied 10X!
1. LEVERAGE	Investment Value	$65,000	$650,000	
	Growth Rate	5%	4%	
2. APPRECIATION	Appreciation Growth	$3,250	$26,000	
3. MORTGAGE PAY DOWN	Principal Paid	NA	$8,631	
4. CASH FLOW	Rental Income	NA	$0	
5. TAX BENEFIT	Tax Savings	NA	$10,000	
	1 Year Return	$3,250	$44,631	
	Annual Growth Rate	5%	29%	

Difference: **$41,381**/year **$3,448**/month!

Why Real Estate is the Safest Investment you can make!

The whole point to investing in any asset is to not just create wealth but to **also** create non-employment or retirement income. It is this non-employment income that you will eventually rely on for financial security and retirement. The security and stability of this income is critical to you, especially in your Senior years. Below is a chart showing California's 25-year rent history starting in 1990. The first thing to notice is the stability of the rental income, as you can see there is a nice steady upward trajectory with little exception. You can research this further by going to UScensus.gov and track rental history by state. What you are going to find is rents have had the

same consistent inflationary growth dating back to 1940! What other asset can say this? The answer is none.
Second critical point- real estate is the only asset that operates on **two separate** supply and demand components. The first supply and demand component is the supply and demand to purchase real estate.
Example; Let's compare how stocks fared with real estate during the great recession of 2008. Let's say you had one million dollars in the stock market when the financial meltdown hit and your million-dollar stock portfolio dropped by 50% to $500,000 dollars in asset value.

What do you think happened to your retirement income? Did it go down? Of course it did, dollar for dollar, 50% of your retirement income is now gone. Let's say you had $5,000 a month of retirement income coming in on that $ 1 million that you had invested in the stock market. It is now only $2,500. Is that a problem if you are retired? For most people this is a huge problem.

Now, let's compare that to real estate. Let's say, you had a million-dollar triplex generating the same $5,000 a month in rent and the economy tanks like it did in 2008 and now no one is buying real estate and the value of your triplex drops to only $500,000.

Did your rents go down in half?

History says no! As you can see on the chart in fact rents actually went up in 2008!

Why?

Even though the demand to purchase real estate declined dramatically in 2008-09 when prices came down by 40-50% the demand for rents went up. The reason the demand went up is because of all the people that were losing their homes. What are the options for someone that is being foreclosed on?

Rent or go homeless?

Not surprisingly, most went out and rented.
The reason real estate is the safest investment you can make is because it is the only asset that you can invest in that operates on **two separate supply and demand components**. The second supply and demand component being the demand to rent real estate.

This is why real estate in high rental demand areas like California and New York are the most secure investment when it comes to investment income. What do you think the chances are that you are going to see rents in your community go down? In most of the US people are moving in and particularly in states like California where they are coming from all over the world!
Do you believe you are going to see this change in your lifetime?
I don't, this is why real estate is the fastest and safest path to wealth and investment income!

(DISCLAIMER: Every investment, including real estate, has a financial risk associated with it due to market fluctuations and the specific individual investment. All information and calculations provided by the Mark 1 Wealth Academy and its financial calculators are deemed to be accurate but are not guaranteed. It is strongly recommended that you seek a second opinion from your CPA or other financial advisor before making any financial investment decisions.)

Chapter Four

The Science of Building Wealth

"Learning is the beginning of wealth."
-Jim Rohn, business philosopher and life strategist

There are seven principles to the science of building wealth which include the five economic benefits of real estate. It is the mastery of these seven principles that can make the difference between massive wealth growth and financial loss. In 2008 we had the greatest financial meltdown in both the stock market and real estate markets. This financial meltdown was very predictable, in fact it was so predictable that I did 13 news media interviews warning consumers of the impending foreclosure crisis.

My point is this, if you know the dynamics of the economy, your local real estate market and the science of building wealth that I am about to review with you in this chapter, you can make money in virtually any environment. Very often you will hear someone say the key to investing is market timing. I disagree, market timing applies if you are buying and selling assets/properties at the median market value like the other novice investors. But if you are a master of the science of building wealth you can anticipate greater opportunities and take advantage of them. The key to making money is not limited to market timing, it is instead in finding an investment that provides a great return on investment. This can be accomplished in 90% of the markets and is generally easier to find in an adverse market. Always remember the greater the crisis, the greater the opportunity!

The First Principle: Leverage

If leverage is a new term it originates in the term *lever*. Think about the lever as a tool. A lever's purpose is to help us lift things beyond our strength limit. The principle of using a lever to lift things beyond our strength limit also applies to growing wealth beyond our own limitations, such as job income.

We've all heard the expression *It takes money to make money*. The saying implies that wealthy people have money already and therefore the power to earn more money, right? Well, not exactly. It does take money to make money, but it doesn't necessarily have to be *your money*. The wealthy understand the power of levering their· money by using other people's money to create wealth. This way they make money on both their money *and* the levered money. Did you know you can do this, too?

Let's say you have $ 10,000 in your 401k and are earning 5% on it. This means you would earn $500 for the year.

But what if you levered your $10,000 into $100,000 and earned 5%? You would earn $5,000 for the year, or 10 times more!

Now, you might ask where is the other $90,000 going to come from? There are many lenders that will loan you the money if you have a satisfactory credit score. Your score doesn't have to be perfect. Now, here's the best part. Say you could get someone else to make the payments on your levered money so the cost of the loan to you is **free**. That's right. Free!

You are probably asking "Why would anyone make the payments on my loan?" The answer is they would do this if there is a value or utility to them. Your investment will provide that utility.

Is this risky?

There is no investment that is completely risk-free. Financial consultants help investors decide between high and low risk investments. If you are a beginning investor it is best to choose an investment where you can mitigate risk. We can do this by constraining the risks through metric tolerances. In simple terms, this means we limit the risk by making sure we have the rental income necessary to cover the payment and expenses of the property and levered money. There are different strategies that you can use with leverage with varying degrees of risk. Your and my tolerance for risk may be different so be sure that you are crystal clear on the risk you are considering when investing using leverage. Age is a critical component to determining your exposure to leverage. The older you are the less leverage you should use.

I strongly encourage you to have a consultation with an expert Real Estate Wealth Advisor before making any final investment decision. Now let's learn how to measure the success of your investment with levered money.

Principle 2: Growth Rate

Growth rate is just what it sounds like: the rate at which your investment is growing. Savvy investors talk about their growth rate or ROI (return on investment) probably more than any other aspect of investing. The reason is because the growth rate is like the score of a game. It dictates whether you are winning or losing the game.

Understanding the dynamics of how growth rate is affected by market conditions and investment strategies is critical to financial success.

There are many factors that affect **growth rate** or **ROI**.

1. One essential factor is the current economy, also known as "**market conditions**". While most people see a weak economy as a bad time to invest history shows us otherwise. A weak economy softens the market place, which means that everything goes on sale. Very often this is the perfect time to buy or invest.

2. **Understanding the tax implications of an investment is another way to maximize ROI.** In the Tax Cuts and Jobs Act of 2017 the tax advantages of real estate where greatly enhanced. Always remember it is important that you discuss tax planning with your CPA or other tax expert. Fortunately, real estate investments are some of the most forgiving in regards to taxes. The IRS can even help you keep your returns on your real estate investments.

3. **Leverage & cash flow management.** We discussed leverage under Principle 1 above and cash flow management is discussed in the chapter "Healthy Spending Habits".

Many investors struggle to earn 6% return on their investment. The earnings on real estate can be significantly more. Savvy real estate investors using the above wealth building principles can are earn in excess of double digit returns compounded annually for many years.

Principle 3: Debt Management

Good Debt vs. Bad Debt

You may have heard of the concepts of good and bad debt and wondered, when is debt a good thing?

Debt is good when it creates *more income* than it costs. Many people never experience the benefits of good debt.

The reason is that many people don't think of their financial future the way the wealthy do. The average person goes through life with a myopic view of their life. They go to work, get a paycheck, and spend it. They don't think in terms of the big picture of their financial life and part of earning good debt is planning.

So what is the big picture? The big picture for the wealthy is not only tracking their monthly bills but also creating passive income that adds to their steady income. You see, in order to reach financial security and retirement **you need non-employment or investment income to exceed your monthly expenses.** Everyone pays attention to what they get paid from their job but many do not pay any attention to the concept of creating non-employment income. Non-employment income is just as critical to your financial security and future as your employment income.

To key to financial security and building wealth is not complicated, it is about two numbers;

How much money is going out and how much money is coming in. This is why a debt management plan is so important. If you are already in debt, you need to have a debt management plan to pay it off so that you can earn a profit.

If all your income goes to paying off old purchases, you cannot really enjoy and earn wealth. To learn how to set up a debt management program (and other good advice) see my chapter on Healthy Spending Habits.

Always remember, it is a person's bills that keep them from retiring. The lower their bills, the sooner they will be able to retire.

Principle 4: Investment Income

How can you establish retirement income that will never run out?
When it comes to retirement in America today, most people fall into one of three categories.

1. The top 10% that have plenty of wealth
2. Those that work for the government in some capacity and have an excellent retirement plan
3. Everyone else.

The overwhelming majority of people rely on the "save and hope" it all works out strategy. Many never know how much money they will need to secure retirement. Very often the idea of having enough money to create retirement income that will never run out is impossible for them. This belief is simply not true, in fact the majority of people in America today can create retirement income that will never run out through real estate. But because very few ever meet with a Real Estate Wealth Advisor they never learn what is possible for their financial future through real estate.

If you want to retire, it is critical that you calculate how much money you will be able to save for retirement at your projected savings rate. You must also calculate what your projected monthly expenses will be at the time of retirement. Once you have determined what these two numbers are you can then determine if you have retirement income that will never run out.

The sad truth is very few people have secure retirement income that will never run out. Instead, they struggle to stretch every dollar they can and very often have to work at least part time their entire life.

All of this doom and gloom about the state of retirement may scare you. **But don't worry. You hold all the knowledge and tools you need in your hands.** By studying and mastering the seven principles of the Science of Building Wealth you can build your wealth and retirement income by more than triple your 401 k or IRA in the stock market. Furthermore, the principles will not only help you retire but help set an example of intelligent financial planning that your family can learn from and apply for generations.

Principle 5: Taxation

Benefiting from Tax Laws

The number one area of wealth growth that the rich understand far better than the average person is taxation. The tax code is a gigantic book of thousands of tax laws. The truth about taxation is that it's really controlled in Washington. Lobbyists influence congress to create tax deductions that will benefit their respective constituency. Tax laws are not common knowledge and explain why a significant portion of the population is not taking advantage of tax laws to get ahead of the system.

The average person has no idea what the tax laws are in their state or how to position themselves best to minimize their income taxes and or increase their rate of return on their investments. Tax laws can be ridiculously complicated so having a knowledgeable CPA (certified public accountant) to work with is critical.

Do you think the wealthy know which investments receive preferred tax status?

You can bet your bottom dollar they know.

Did you know that not all investments are treated the same by the IRS?

The average person doesn't know that investments are not all created equal according to the IRS. Many people save what they can in their retirement account thinking they are doing the smart thing because their retirement savings is tax deferred. The downside to tax deferred accounts is that you will still be paying ordinary income taxes when you withdraw your earnings at the time of retirement. What this means is approximately one third of your life savings is NOT your money, it is instead the governments money. These taxes severely affect your investment return adversely, thereby lowering your return on investment.

What if your investment benefitted from some taxes?

One of the most favored investment classes for taxation is real estate. Whether it be a home or rental property, the

IRS has tax deductions that actually increase return on investment instead of lowering it!

As the years go by these tax write-offs add significantly to returns in dollars and ROI. Some of the tax deductions are mortgage interest, property taxes, and depreciation to name a few. Another huge tax advantage that real estate has is the ability to sell an investment and NOT pay the capital gains tax by replacing the investment property using a 1031 Tax Deferred Exchange. I'll describe how to get the exchange in the chapter "The Formula". This ability to replace small investment properties over and over with larger investments allows you the ability to accelerate your wealth growth.

Principle 6: Protecting Your Life Savings/Assets

It takes years of hard work, discipline and planning to accumulate the wealth we need to protect our families and secure our retirement. But it can all disappear in a flash with one calamity, whether it be with a major economic collapse or a tragic accident. Protecting our assets is just as critical as accumulating them. There are many perils can that can devastate a lifetime of assets.

Dangers to Beware

Legal liability can be detrimental to your wealth. The personal liability from a car accident caused by an individual or their family member could cause them to lose everything. Talk to an attorney or insurance agent and they can tell you horror story after horror story about people that were wiped out by legal liability. In all things financial, the importance of mitigating risk and taking calculated risks will protect you. Legal risks are not the kind you want to take. Make sure you cover your assets.

Creditors

Another major concern is creditors. Now none of us plan on having creditors pursuing us to pay our bills but through the years I have seen people come on hard times due to a job layoff, economic collapse or medical crisis. They build up a large debt load trying to keep their head above water and then the dam breaks and the creditors begin pursuing them. Judgments are issued and then the creditors come after the assets. The simple solution is to always, *always* pay your bills as soon as you can before creditors come after you.

Hire legal help

You can protect your assets with a bulletproof legal protection plan. You will need quality professional legal help. Trust attorneys are a good place to start. A good estate attorney can also help with understanding the benefits of using corporations and or Limited Liability Companies to protect assets. I will go into each of these subjects in detail in later chapters.

What can go wrong legally?

The short answer is a lot. The more assets you accumulate the more of a target that you become for lawsuits, whether they are justified or not! Legalized extortion is one potential problem where someone with assets is sued with the objective of settling with the plaintiff/attorney. Since the cost of legal fees would be more than settling most people will settle the lawsuit.

Many people with wealth form corporations with the state with the specific purpose of making it impossible for attorneys to identify your assets. I'll go into this in the last chapter, "Protect Your Investments".

I want to encourage you to follow through on your investments and protect them fiercely. There are few things worse than spending a life time building your wealth and then losing it all due to some unforeseen and unanticipated disaster.

Principle 7: Risk Management

When is the best time to invest?

All investors struggle with the question of when to invest and when to wait. There are many factors to consider when analyzing the risk of an investment. But the key is economics 101- Supply and Demand. Let's review:

1. **The State of the Economy:** We all love the idea of catching the market when the economy is at its lowest point with demand thereby offering the best prices possible for our investment. The problem with this is the only time to know for sure is years later when there is some distance and perspective to accurately analyze market timing. Consequently, most people either never invest or their market

timing objective is off because they have waited way to long.

2.   Herd Investing: There is an old expression in investing that goes "Trend is your friend." The majority of people follow this philosophy of waiting until they see the herd of people taking the leap to invest in a strong economic market climate. This philosophy rarely pays off because demand is so strong very often there are bidding wars for properties.

3.   **Contrarian Investing:** Investing when others are not. Baron Rothschild has a famous quote: "The time to invest is when there is blood in the streets." Contrarian investing is when the market is on sale because people who were not prepared for the market downturn are now selling because they need the cash and they need it now. If you examine Warren Buffet's history of investing, you will learn it is more active when the economy is weak.

4. **Buy and Sell Investing:** There are a lot of people that like the thrill of the chase. Investing is like gambling to them. They place their bet down on an investment at one price and hope their investment knowledge will prove to be right. They sell quickly and hope for a gain. Short term investing or flipping is much harder for the average Joe. I am not a believer in this type of investing. The reason is it requires a massive amount of time, the time to find a good priced property, the time to rehab and manage the project etc. The reality in my mind is you have created another job. A job that will stop providing income as soon as you stop finding and rehabbing properties. This is not a wealth building strategy to financial security and retirement strategy.

Investing for the Long Term

The simple truth is that none of us has a crystal ball that will guarantee our· investment timing is perfect. The smart strategy is to make quality investments that will consistently increase in value and cash flow over the long haul. If quality investments are made and retained over long terms, the market timing almost becomes irrelevant as a portfolio of investments grows.

The Single Rule

The single most important difference between the rich and everyone else is what they know about the dynamics of wealth growth. Mastering the science of building wealth and the fundamental principles of wealth growth will provide a foundation for your wealth-building journey. To begin your journey schedule a meeting with an expert Real Estate Wealth Advisor! Don't try to go it alone. Find an expert that understands what your wealth building objectives are and get a custom wealth building plan prepared.

Chapter Five

Buying a Home is Your Key to Retirement

"There is something permanent, and something extremely profound, in owning a home." – Kenny Guinn, Former Governor of Nevada

Home buying can save you thousands in the future by buying now and watching your housing costs go down. Don't throw money away on rent. Spend it on an investment that will give you equity, stability, and put money towards your future.

Buying is Better than Renting

Many people rent because they simply don't believe they can afford a mortgage. This is a common result of misinformation and the lack of faith in financial mobility in low-income communities that I discussed in Chapter Two. Here are the best reasons to quit renting:

- **Rental payments go up. Mortgages eventually end.** As we saw earlier, rent payments increase steadily, making it harder to save for a mortgage, your children's college tuition and your eventual retirement. When you own, your real estate could triple in value over 30 years. When you rent, there is no "up side." You do not have assets that accrue in value as you pay the mortgage down. You lose all of the tax write-offs that come with owning a home and your "out of pocket" payments could be much higher too.

• **Inflation benefits homeowners:** The value of homes in California has consistently increased through the years and, the few times when property values have decreased, it wasn't long before property values recovered and more than made up for any value reductions. As inflation rises, so does the value of your home. Home renovations and design improvements often qualify as tax write-offs and can further increase the value of your home when you sell it – usually at a much higher price.

• **Your retirement depends on your living situation:** Keeping up with inflation is a struggle when looking to save for retirement. This is especially true when it comes to housing. Many people are unable to retire when they would like to because they must continue paying rent or keeping up their mortgage payments. Buying sooner rather than later can help you prepare for retirement by increasing your net worth, getting rid of one huge payment, and giving you stability.

Rules of Retirement:

Social Security has become the retirement lifeline for many people. The other challenge with funding retirement is life expectancy, which has increased to about 80 years old, and is expected to grow. If you would like to retire at 65 years old, fifteen years is a long time to live on investment income, or savings.

If you don't come from a family of wealth and you don't learn how much to save for retirement in school -- how are you going to prepare yourself? Largely, financial planners will suggest buying stocks and bonds that come with either a risky likelihood of profits, or a stable but very low return. For a future of financial security, you need to make a realistic estimation on one question:

How much monthly income will I need to retire?

This number depends on how far out retirement is for you. If you are 25 and planning to retire in 40 years, you are going to need much more than a 45 year-old person saving for retirement 20 years out.

Other things to consider:

If I retire at 60 to 65 years-old, how much will I need considering inflation increases? Another factor in retirement is housing - will you have a home paid off? Will you be renting? Will you have mortgage payment? This is where home buying comes in and its long-term benefits.

Sit down with a calculator.

Let's use today's dollars as an example. Make accurate estimates so that you can actually enjoy your retirement. Even if you just plan spending time with family members, save enough so you can continue some of the lifestyle elements you enjoy today, such as allocating money for dinner and a movie or for a vacation once in a while. Let's assume you decide you will need $5,000 a month during your retirement. Now, how much money do you need to accumulate in investments to secure that income? That depends on your rate of return and what kind of investments you have. As you become older, your investments need to become more conservative so that they're less at risk for severe market changes. As an example, if you have one million dollars invested and you get a 6% return, then that one million will give $60,000 per year. Divide that by 12 months and that gets you your $5,000 a month. My point is that most people grossly underestimate how much money they need to accumulate so that they can have enough income to provide a comfortable lifestyle and to last long enough for their extended life.

Roadblocks: Inflation & Wages

For the past 100 years, the average annual inflation rate has been 3.22 percent. Inflation is a perpetual factor of the economy. One hundred years ago the volatility of inflation was much worse, spurring the invention of the Federal Reserve. The primary objective of the Reserve was to smooth out the big swings in the economy so we didn't have as many run ups and collapses.

In the recession of 2008, the Federal Reserve Chairman Ben Bernanke, an expert on the Great Depression, dropped interest rates to historic lows in an effort to stabilize the economy and avoid a collapse of the market and another great depression. The regulation of inflation is one of the primary roles of the Federal Reserve. Inflation is not an accident, it is by design. The objective of the Federal Reserve is to stimulate economic growth. Inflation is a part of that growth process. Raising and lowering interest rates is the fuel and brake to the national economy. The rich understand the power of inflation and the need to have assets to keep pace. Inflation has always been here and will always be here. It is critical to understand how to get inflation to work for you and not against you when planning for the future and estimating the income you will need.

The slow increase of wages is the main reason that so many Americans struggle to stabilize financial security in their present and future. Having an income that puts food on the table does not equate to a stable future. People need to earn enough wages so that they can invest and accumulate assets. If you do not have enough wages to ever invest, you can never get ahead. The average middle-income earner is looking forward to these pay raises, but the truth is that with every pay raise they are barely getting ahead.

Is inflation an ally or an enemy? The answer lies whether inflation is applied to assets or not. The most reliable way to get ahead financially is through assets. How do you accumulate relatively low-risk assets with potential for long-term return? You know the answer by now — real estate investing.

How to Save for a Down Payment:

Saving for a down payment can feel like a big financial undertaking, but I promise you, it will be worth it. Even though this quest may seem stressful, know that achieving the financial security that you desire is possible. The amount of money that you will need for a down payment can be far less than you might imagine. There are many first time buyer programs with very low down payments and some that include a grant to cover ALL of the down payment and closing costs. Yes, that's right. You can buy a home with little or no money with the right first time loan program. We will review some of those programs next. If you are not eligible for a very low down or grant program it will be critical that you be able to save for your down payment and closing costs. To do this you must make saving money your number one priority. Find an account at your current bank or a new one where you can store your savings and will not be tempted (or allowed) to touch for any reason except your down payment on your home purchase. Learn how to prioritize saving first on your budget. If you can have your employer take a percentage of your net pay and put into a savings account do it. We can almost always learn to live on less. It is these sacrifices and self-discipline that will make the difference in you being able to achieve your financial security. To become a homeowner is to fulfill part of the American dream, and the down payment is the first key step that you need to make.

How much will you need for a down payment?

There are many low down payment options for purchasing your first home, if you qualify. These options may include a 3.5% down payment that can be provided by a grant for you, meaning you have a No Down Payment Home Loan. We will review some of the low-down-payment programs. Fannie Mae and Freddie Mac say they will now buy mortgages with as little as 3% down, a nice drop from the old 5% minimum.

Even though it's easier to get loans now that down payment requirements have been reduced, there's still the matter of how to save not only for a down payment, but for closing costs. Something to also keep in mind is that home ownership comes with other expenses such as inevitable repairs and maintenance costs. But don't worry -- being a homeowner will pay off.

Chapter Six

Begin with a Budget

The first thing you need to do to prepare for your first home is save.

Open a Savings Account

The best way to build a down payment is to save in advance by using accounts or investments that earn interest, that are not easily accessible (that you're not tempted to touch), and don't put your funds at risk. Do not put your down payment money into a checking account, or any debit card account that you carry on you, or hidden in a safe deposit box. That's counterproductive because it will earn little to no interest, and it is too easy to dip into when Christmas or some other event comes rolling around.

Start a Budget

The easy to way to establish a budget is by using a spreadsheet. Google Docs offers free budget templates. Take advantage of them by doing some simple searching around on the web. The spreadsheet should show your monthly gross income (and your spouse's if you are planning to purchase the house together). Then, show what you pay for other monthly costs such as rent, student loans, car payments, and credit card bills. Subtract these costs from your net income. How much money is left each month? And how do you spend it? Start keeping receipts for things such as gasoline, utilities, restaurants, entertainment, parking, and other things you spend money on. You can also find this information by going through your online bank statements.

You will learn where your money goes, how much you take in and how much goes out. Now you need to look through with this question in mind: Where can costs be cut?

Since wages increase at a slow crawl and you are trying to increase your net income by buying a home in the first place, there's probably not an excess of money left over after expenses. This means that the only way to get ahead is to bring in more money or change your spending habits (meaning spend *less*) and look aggressively for new ways to save.

This may seem difficult, but the reality is that almost every household can save more, and if you're truly on the path to wealth and financial strength, you need to learn how to do this. The good news is that starting is the tough part, but once you get going it can be so rewarding you will be beefed up with pride at what's in your bank account. A quote I love on savings is "By definition, saving for anything requires us to not get things now so that we can get bigger ones later." – Jean Chatzky, financial editor for NBC's Today Show. You need to keep your eyes on the prize, and the change in spending habits will be well worth it!

To create savings, especially in the beginning, you must be ruthless. Set a time to review your spending and budget, say the first and third Mondays of every month. Go through the numbers with zeal, asking if every nickel and dime was justified. Be blunt with yourself about your choices and question the motive. Did you need to valet park or could you afford to have a little patience?

Check Interest Rates

Interest rates differ between credit cards, savings accounts, car loans, and other accounts, Go through your every bill and check the interest rate. Can you get a better one?

For instance, if you've been making full and prompt credit card payments, call up the credit card company and ask them for a lower rate. You'd be surprised what you can get simply by asking. You could save yourself hundreds of dollars (depending on the amount of your debt) simply by asking for a more affordable rate, getting you closer to your down payment.

Auto loans are a little different. If you have a car loan with simple interest, then it might make sense to prepay the debt. However, many auto loans use a special "sum-of-the-digits" interest calculation, which makes prepayments less attractive as well as very difficult to understand.

Consider selling your current vehicle and getting a used one. This option is not always feasible given trade-in values and sum-of-the-digits financing, but run the numbers and always consider safety first. Meanwhile, when you get a car next, make sure it's financed with simple interest and has a strong warranty that will cover repairs even if you move. Also, if you have savings, you can put more money down and qualify for a lower rate — still another reason to bulk up your savings accounts.

Check Your Credit

Your ability to borrow—and the interest rate you will pay—are closely dependent on your credit score. Lenders might be very willing to originate a mortgage for you with little down and less savings if you have strong credit. Your credit score is based on the credit reports, electronic files which show such things as where you have credit accounts, how much you have borrowed, your total debt, any missed or late payments, and how much more you can borrow with existing accounts.

"The key to the system is the assumption that credit reports are accurate, but that's not always the case," according to Rick Sharga, executive vice president at Auction.com. "Sometimes credit reports are wrong, and when that happens your credit standing can be demolished. The result will be either higher borrowing costs or maybe no mortgage or auto loan at all."

According to the Federal Trade Commission about 20% of all credit reports have errors. Five percent have mistakes that can drop scores by 25 points. That's enough to move marginal borrowers into lower credit categories and higher rates.

Even worse, one report in every 250 has so many errors that the borrower's score is actually off at least 100 points. That's enough to sink a lot of mortgage applications and move your credit status from gold to tin.

The only solution is to check your report for factual errors and out-of-date items several months before you apply for a mortgage or car loan—enough time to clean up errors and disputes.

Saving Step-by-Step

Spending less is the most efficient and consistent way to reach your savings goals, but there's also another source of savings—those occasional events that bring extra money into your household. Think of birthdays, bonuses, tax refunds, and getting married. While it can be tempting to splurge with these periodic windfalls, this is money that can be used to increase your savings account quickly without dipping into regular income.

Gifts

In the rare situation that someone you know would offer to pay you a large portion of the down payment there is some protocol you need to look into to protect yourself legally in case a family feud or change-of-heart occurs. To be recognized as a "gift," the donor will have to sign a gift letter saying there's no expectation of repayment, interest, or anything else.

Loan programs, especially loans insured by the FHA, want down payment money to come directly from borrowers to demonstrate financial responsibility and an ability to save. Because loan programs make a distinction between down payment money and other dollars -- say a "seller contribution" used to pay closing costs — it's ideal to get as much down payment cash as you can. If getting a hefty down payment saved up in time is not possible, read the chapter Buyers Assistance Programs for a slew of incredible options for you.

Chapter Seven

The Formula

You're ready to buy a house. You've sat with a loan officer. You've prequalified for a loan. You know how much you need to save for a down payment, or you know whether your payment is covered by a grant or other assistance program. You're ready to go and select the first house.

Let's walk through this three-step process of how you can accomplish two goals:

1. Accumulate wealth with a stable, growing income

2. Accumulate enough monthly income to be financially independent through retirement

Step One

Step 1- Purchasing your first property. There are many loan programs available to assist you in purchasing your first property. For this case study we will use an FHA loan with a 3.5% down payment and a $300,000 purchase price. The down payment is going to be $10,500. Your closing costs are $3,000 approximately and will be paid for through the loan or by the seller. You decide to purchase the property with the hope that it appreciates at least 5% per year (5% is the national appreciation average). Congratulations!

You've reached the first goal and purchased a home and made it your primary residence.

Step Two – Property #2

The next objective is to save enough money for a down payment to purchase your next property. We must analyze what is a realistic amount that you can save every month. Our goal is to make your second purchase within 5 to 7 years. Hypothetically, let's say that you can save $500 a month. Over 60 months this will accumulate to $30,000. At this pace of savings, you will be able to buy a second property within five years. The rate of your first property's appreciation will vary based on market conditions. In California, the historical average appreciation rate for residential real estate from 1968-2014 was 7.3%. This appreciation rate includes three different recessions and of course includes the most recent real estate meltdown. For this case study we will use a 5% appreciation rate. The appreciation that you earn may be another option to assist you with your down payment for your second property. There are two issues you want to be concerned with before you borrow money on your first purchase to make your second purchase. The first is the cash flow for the first property when you rent it. The other is the ability to qualify for a new home loan to purchase property two. A negative cash flow on the first property will impact your ability to purchase property two so be sure to be pre-qualified by a competent lender.

Using a 5% appreciation rate will mean that your first property purchase will now have a market value of approximately $380,000. The second step is to make a lateral move, meaning that you are buying a property of similar value. This does not mean that you cannot buy a nicer or more expensive property if you can qualify for a larger loan and have been able to save the down payment to accomplish this due to a significant increase in your income. However, for most people, that is not possible so, for this case study, we will use the more conservative assumption of making a lateral purchase.

Now you can buy property #2. We turn property #1 into a rental and the objective is to rent it for more than what your monthly payments are so that you can make the mortgage/property tax bills and have money left over for any costs that may occur (improvements or repairs). If you have accomplished this, then congratulations. You have successfully completed Step Two.

The Mistake That Everyone Makes With Step Two - Property #2

People very often make the mistake of cashing in early. I speak more about this in Healthy Spending Habits- a must-read chapter if you want to develop the tools and habits to accumulate wealth successfully.

Many people make the mistake of selling the primary residence to buy the largest property possible. The big psychological adjustment that this strategy requires for you to achieve the financial security that we all want is to NOT sell your first property purchased. Virtually every property owner wants to sell their first property and roll all their equity into purchasing the largest second property possible. This is a HUGE mistake! There is no doubt that all the equity that you have built up in your first purchase will be very tempting to use as a down payment on a bigger nicer property, but don't do it! There is nothing more important than this one disciplined financial move to put you on your way to financial security and retirement.

There are three problems with buying a big house. The first is the increased costs which include a bigger mortgage payment, bigger property tax bill, higher utility bills, higher maintenance costs, etc. The second problem is a larger residence will never generate retirement income. The third is the total asset value that you will have. Let's say that you sell your first property for a price of $380,000 and purchase a new larger property for $500,000. Compare that to keeping the first property, which is now worth $380,000 and buying a new property for $380,000, your combined total asset value would then be $760,000. This increased asset value is going to dramatically accelerate your ability to accumulate wealth. This can be a tough decision to make but it comes down to a very basic question: What is more important? Your financial security, or impressing your friends with a big house?

Let's assume you have overcome the overwhelming desire to buy a bigger house and have chosen to secure your financial future and have purchased your second property for $380,000 with a down payment and closing costs totaling $19,529. In reviewing chart 1 below, you will see an equity build up of over $830,000 over a 20 year period with a return on investment of 4,155%! Imagine turning $19,529 into over $800,000.

Projected Purchase Price	$380,000.00
Down Payment (%)	3.50%
Down Payment ($)	$13,300.00
Closing Costs	$6,229.22
Total Investment	$19,529.22

1st TD Terms

Term (Months)	360
Interest Rate	4.25%
Total Amount Financed	$366,700.00
Monthly Expense (PI)	($1,803.94)

Equity Position Evaluation	
Present Day Value	$380,000.00
Appreciation Rate	5.00%
Duration of Investment (years)	20
Estimated Value after Duration	$1,008,253.13
Loan Balance after Duration	$177,277.90
Equity Position	$830,975.23

Return on Investment	
Total Return ($)	$811,446.00
Total Return (%)	4155.03%
Compounded Rate of Return (%)	20%

Step 3

Seven years after you've bought property #1 (and two years after you bought property #2) you're going to sell property #1 and use a 1031 tax deferred exchange sale.

What is a 1031 Tax Deferred Exchange Sale?

Thanks to IRC Section 1031, a properly structured 1031 exchange allows an investor to sell a property, to reinvest the proceeds in a new property and to defer all capital gain taxes. IRC Section 1031 (a)(1) states:

"No gain or loss shall be recognized on the exchange of property held for productive use in a trade or business or for investment, if such property is exchanged solely for property of like-kind which is to be held either for productive use in a trade or business or for investment."

This means that you can sell your property and buy a "like-kind" and receive no penalty on your capital gains, which is another term for profit from the sale. This is a huge benefit because at the seven-year mark since you've bought your first property, when you sell this property using a 1031 tax deferred exchange sale, you will take the equity from this sale of property #1 and purchase property #3.

At the seven-year mark you will have approximately $171,000 in equity from the sale of property #1. The third step is to sell this property for the market value price of $422,000 using a 1031 tax deferred tax exchange (this is using a 5% appreciation rate).

Projected Purchase Price	$300,000.00
Down Payment (%)	3.50%
Down Payment ($)	$10,500.00
Closing Costs	$5,596.76
Total Investment	$16,096.76

1st TD Terms	
Term (Months)	360
Interest Rate	4.25%
Total Amount Financed	$289,500.00
Monthly Expense (PI)	($1,424.17)

Equity Position Evaluation	
Present Day Value	$300,000.00
Appreciation Rate	5.00%

Duration of Investment (years)	7
Estimated Value after Duration	$422,130.13
Loan Balance after Duration	$251,093.91
Equity Position	$171,036.21

Return on Investment	
Total Return ($)	$154,939.46
Total Return (%)	962.55%
Compounded Rate of Return (%)	37%

Purchasing Property #3

Property #3 will ideally be a duplex or triplex depending on the market value of the properties in your market area. If you hold this property for 20 years, using a 5% appreciation rate will achieve an equity position of $1,374,430. When adding this to the equity from the property #2 purchase, your combined net worth is $2,205,405.

Projected Purchase Price	$600,000.00
Down Payment (%)	25.00%
Down Payment ($)	$150,000.00
Closing Costs	$8,281.88

Total Investment	$158,281.88

1st TD Terms	
Term (Months)	360
Interest Rate	4.25%
Total Amount Financed	$450,000.00
Monthly Expense (PI)	($2,213.73)

Equity Position Evaluation	
Present Day Value	$600,000.00
Appreciation Rate	5.00%
Duration of Investment (years)	20
Estimated Value after Duration	$1,591,978.62
Loan Balance after Duration	$217,548.56
Equity Position	$1,374,430.07

Return on Investment	
Total Return ($)	$1,216,148.19
Total Return (%)	768.34%
Compounded Rate of Return (%)	11%

Now let's say you buy a $600,000 property and put down a 25% down payment that equals $150,0000. You put your down payment on the duplex and now you have two units rented. **Now you're building retirement income. Also,** you have two assets that are appreciating and using the power of inflation, a $600,000 property and a $380,000 property. That's $980,000 in assets that are appreciating. The total of $980,000 in assets is far superior than if you sold the first property and bought a new larger home worth $500,000. By selling the first property and purchasing a larger home, you have severely limited your ability to invest and create wealth. Additionally, you only have one asset that does not create retirement income. By not selling property #1 and making a lateral move. you now have two assets totaling $980,000. Your assets have nearly doubled and you are now generating retirement income. In 20 years, using the 5% appreciation rate, property #2 will have an approximate market value of $1,008,253 with an equity position of $830,000.

Property #3, the duplex, will have a property value of $1,591,978 and you will have $1,374,000 worth equity. When adding this to the equity from the property #2 purchase, your combined net worth is $2,205,405.

When you reach the age of 62 you can eliminate your housing expense by either paying off your mortgage over the years or by refinancing your primary residence into a reverse mortgage. You will still have the duplex creating the income that you need and rents increasing each year to keep up with inflation.

If this sounds exciting to you imagine how much wealth you can accumulate if you keep buying properties.

Chapter Eight

How the Formula Works: Leverage

Leverage is a unique advantage in the investing world. According to Investopedia.com, leverage is:

The use of various financial instruments or borrowed capital (funds borrowed from individuals or institutions) to increase the potential return of an investment.

While this isn't a complete definition, it's a good starting point. Leverage is what allows you to spend a relatively small sum of money, say a $15,000 down payment, and earn a huge return such as a house with a value of $400,000.

That may seem great enough for someone looking to invest in a residence, but look at what happens with leverage in rental properties. By purchasing and renting out properties, someone else will pay the bulk of your mortgage. So not only will you finance your property using little cash, you will be able to pay off a huge sum of your mortgage (if not all) by renting it out. Let me explain further.

OPM

In *Investing in Real Estate*, Gary Eldred introduces the concept of using OPM (Other People's Money) towards your investment. This is one of the most powerful advantages in investing almost unique to real estate alone. Eldred writes:

"Used intelligently, financial leverage (OPM) magnifies your gains. It will increase your cash-on-cash-return, magnify your equity build up (acorns into oak trees), and help you acquire properties that you otherwise could not acquire—if you had to rely exclusively on your own cash balances."

In case it's not obvious, leverage magnifies returns. Over time, properties increase in value. Renting out the property covers the mortgage. It is likely that home appreciation will raise the value of your rental home, and you may be able to increase rent prices. This is how properties are able to generate so much income, because a small deposit earns a long, sustained income, asset, and equity. Now you know how leverage works. But say you have enough money to buy a property all in cash. Is it still wise to use leverage and save yourself a long-term mortgage? See the answer in this example.

Example 1:

You buy a $100,000 rental property and finance (take out a loan) $90,000 of it. You now own and control the property. You rent out the property at rent levels that cover the mortgage. Aside from some necessary home repairs and maintenance costs, the property is paying for itself. Within five few years, due to the natural growth of inflation, your property is now worth $300,000, yet you have put up only 10 percent of the purchase price. You paid $10,000 and receive a $300,000 value in equity which you may choose to apply to a bigger duplex, or another rental property. If you paid $100,000 cash for the property you would not have leveraged your purchase and would not have been able to use OPM to cover the mortgage.

Example 1 is the magic of real estate investing. You might think both pursuits of rental property are equal, but that would be incorrect, which is why leverage is so crucial. By financing much of the property, then filling it with tenants, you offer a service and instead have them pay the property off. Sure, if you saved for who knows how long and lived way below your means, you could have purchased the property in cash and still earned a return. But even if you had the money, it makes more sense to finance it and have the tenants pay for the space (and consequently your mortgage).

If you're not convinced leverage is the best factor behind real estate investing, let's compare the returns over time on five properties. In these examples I will compare investments on a $100,000 property (low by California standards- but let's keep it a round number for simplicity).

The formula we will follow to find the returns are this: Return on Investment (ROI) = Net Operating Income (NOI)/cash investment

Example 2: $100,000 all-cash purchase
ROI = Income (NOI)/cash investment
=10,000/ 100,000
= 10%

In this example, you pocket the full $10,000 of net operating income (gross rental income less vacancy and operating expenses such as insurance, repairs, maintenance, and property taxes). If you instead finance part of your purchase price, you will make mortgage payments on the amount you borrow. If we assume you find financing at 8% for 30 years, you will have to pay your lender $7.34 a month for each $1,000 you borrow. Now, using various percentages of leverage, the following examples show the gains that leverage offers:

Example 3: $50,000 down payment; $50,000 financed. Yearly mortgage payments equal $4,404 (50 x $7.3 4 x 12). Net income after mortgage payments (which is called cash throw-off) equals $5,596 ($10,000 NOI less $4,404). ROI = $5,596/$50000 = 11.1%

Example 4: $25,000 down payment; $75,000 financed. Yearly mortgage payments equal $6,607 (75 x $7.34 x 12). Net income after mortgage payments (cash throw off) equals $3,394 ($10,000 NOI Less $6,606) = 13.6%

Example 5: $10,000 down payment; $90,000 financed. Yearly mortgage payments equal $7,927 (90 x $7.34 x 12). Net income after mortgage payments (cash throw off) equals $2,073. ($10,000 NOI less $7,927). ROI = $2,073/$10,000 = 20.7%

With the figures in these examples, the highly leveraged (90 percent loan-to-value ratio) purchase yields a cash-on-cash return that's double the rate of a cash purchase. In principle, the more you borrow, the less cash you invest in a property, the greater you magnify your returns. The actual rate of return you'll earn on your properties depends on the rents, expenses, interest, rates, and purchase prices that apply to your investment properties. Work through those actual numbers at the time you buy to see how much you can gain (or lose) from leverage.

These calculations do not figure in any profits from another essential investment principle: appreciation.

According to Investopedia.com, appreciation's definition is this:

An increase in the value of an asset over time.

The increase can occur for a number of reasons including increased demand or weakening supply, or as a result of changes in inflation or interest rates. This is the opposite of depreciation, which is a decrease over time. Your property is an asset. As it increases in time it increases in value.

Over the years (if well selected) your investment properties will increase in price. If the price of that $100,000 property we've just discussed increases at an average annual rate of 3 percent, you earn another $3,000 a year. If its price increases at an annual rate of 5 percent, you'll gain $5,000 more a year. And at a 7 percent annual rate of appreciation, your gains will hit $7,000 a year. Add together annual net rental income and annual price gains and you'll earn these total returns:

Total ROI = Income + Appreciation/ Cash investment
Example 1: $100,000 all-cash purchase and (a) 3 percent, (b) 5 percent, and (c) 7 percent rates of appreciation

With appreciation included in the calculation your returns would be this:

Example 1: $100,000 all cash purchase and (a) 3 percent, (b) 5 percent, and (c) 7 percent rates of appreciation:

Total ROI = 17%

Example 4: $100,000 down payment and (a) 3 percent, (b) 5 percent, and (c) 7 percent rates of appreciation.

(a) Total ROI- $2,073 + $3,000/$10,000 = 50.7%

If you're concerned about not benefiting from appreciation rates and you're a Californian resident, you'll be happy to hear this: **California has a history of higher appreciation rates than the rest of the country. Why?**

Housing in California has been more expensive than most of the rest of the country for decades. But in 1970, the gap between California's home prices and the rest of the country began to widen even further. California home prices went from 30 percent above U.S. levels to more than 80 percent higher. This trend has continued. Currently, an average California home costs $400,000 -- about 2.5 times the average national home price ($180,000 at the time this was written). California's rent coincides with this: the average monthly rent is about $1,240 -- 50% higher than the rest of the country.

Risks of Leverage

Like any wise investor you should be asking, so what are the risks? Many real estate gurus have made a healthy buck or two off of selling "get rich quick" real estate schemes. Most of these successful "gurus" lead their followers astray by not warning them of the risks of leverage. Listen closely now: **Highly leveraged real estate magnifies the risks as well as returns**. The only way to ensure profits and minimize losses on your investments is to take caution. Here are some perfect examples of leverage gone wrong and what silly mistakes you won't be making:

Hope for the Best, Prepare for the Worst

Unfortunately, many inexperienced and naive real estate investors have failed at successful investing. The failure comes most often to investors that dream of unrealistic and overly optimistic expectations for the market values of their properties. They expect them to increase steadily in gains of 10 to 20 percent a year, outrageously high percentages to be expecting. Would you expect your paycheck to increase year after year at that rate? These dreamers have often lost touch with reality because they've been preached to incorrectly, or they have gotten too optimistic out of excitement for their venture.

The Do-Nots of Real Estate Investing:

1. Do not get distracted by the promise of returns -- it's not a promise it is a likelihood. You need to prepare for the possibility of little to no appreciation.

2. Do not overlook a purchase price and *assume* that it will increase exponentially in value, justifying a higher price. Be economical and careful with what you sign up for. Only bite off what you can chew.

3. Do not let rent levels drop below the mortgage if you can help it. Your strategy is only successful if the property earns as much or as close as you can get to covering its mortgage. If you cannot get it at

exactly mortgage coverage, look into adding value to increase rent levels.

One example of what not to do.

One investor buys a $300,000 four-plex with a payment of $30,000. After property operating expenses and mortgage payments, the investor faced a negative cash flow of $1,000 a month. The investor thought that it was nothing to worry because the future selling price would be up 15 percent a year. Based on his expected rate of gain, here's how the investor calculated annual returns that he (unrealistically) expected:

ROI= Income + Appreciation/Cash Investment

= $12,000 (12x$1,000) + $45,000 (.15 x 300,000) / $30,000

= $33,000/ $30,000

= 110%

This optimistic investor could not afford to spend $1,000 monthly income on his investment. He fell behind mortgage payments. As the market slowed, he could not sell or refinance the property. The lender foreclosed. The investor lost the property, his down payment of $30,000, the $24,000 of monthly negative cash shortfalls that he had covered prior to default, and his once-high credit score.

This example is not to scare you. Instead, it should remind you to keep your expectations reasonable, which I have shown at a variety of rates, as well as providing add-value strategies and techniques to minimize losses. This poor investor did not consider his purchase price, nor reasonable rent levels to cover that mortgage, and he lost his four-plex because of it.

The four lessons to take away from this investor's regrettable (yet common and perfectly avoidable) mistakes:

1. Never expect the value of any investment (gold, stocks, antiques, real estate) **to increase by 10, 15, or 20 percent year after year**. If you need high rates of price gain to make your investment attractive, you set yourself up for a big risk and big losses.

2. Avoid negative cash flows. If the income from an asset does not support the price paid, you magnify your risk and chance of loss. Think of it like hiring an employee. You need an employee to earn their cost in order for your business to become profitable. As negative cash flows increase, the probability of severe price correction looms large.

3. Beware of financial overreach. High leverage (high loan-to-value ratio) usually requires large mortgage payments relative to the amount of net income that a property brings in. Even if at first you don't suffer negative cash flows, many other issues can push you into negative cash flows (also called an alligator). Vacancies, higher-than-expected expenses, or large rent concessions intended to attract good tenants can temporarily lead you into dangerous waters. This is one more reason to remember why saving is so essential to building wealth. It's not just your wealth, it's your safety net.

Over a period of 10 to 20 years, real estate will grow your net worth many times over. But to enjoy that long-term future you must pass through cyclical downturns. Without cash reserves to defend against unforeseen droughts, you may be pulled into negative cash flows that can destroy the equity you've earned and ruin the work accomplished to get there before you find safety in (reserves and high) numbers.

4. Even when the property financing looks good, avoid overpaying for a property. Investors whose expectations are too optimistic buy overpriced properties with little or no down payment deals. In the earlier four-plex example, the investor agreed to pay $300,000 for the four-plex, not because the property income justified the $300,000. He paid it because he was excited about the idea of easy credit, low payment financing. Compared with the

$600,000 sales price he expected to reap after a few years, his purchase price looked cheap.

This is not to say that you should not take advantage of buyer's assistance programs or desirable financing. It is to say one should consider the possible setbacks of high loans to value.

To manage the risks of highly leveraged OPM, adopt these six safeguards:

1. Buy bargain-priced properties. You can build a financial parachute into your deals when you pay less than market value or pay less than a property is worth.

2. Buy properties that you can profitably improve. To build your net worth more quickly and reduce the risk of leverage, add value to properties through creativity, sweat, equity, remodeling, and renovation. This will not only add personalized touches making the space (ideally) more attractive to renters, it will increase your selling price later on down the line.

3. Buy properties with below-market rents that you can raise to market levels within a relatively short time. (6-12 months). Increase your rental income and as a percentage of net operating income (NOI), your mortgage payments will become easier to pay. You will enjoy a larger margin of safety.

4. Buy properties with low interest rate financing such as mortgage assumptions, adjustable rate mortgages, interest rate, buy downs, or seller financing. Low interest rates help you manage high debt. High interest rates make debt less affordable—especially beware of low interest rates that may disappear within just a few years (or less).

5. Buy right time, right price, right place properties. "All real estate is local" is an oft-cited cliché that contains a kernel of truth. Various neighborhoods and cities offer unique differences with respect to price, location, and market timing. To reduce risk and increase rewards, proactively study and select from such opportunities.

6. When high leverage presents an anxious level of risk, increase your down payment to lower your loan-to-value ratio and lower your monthly mortgage payments. If available cash does not permit a higher down payment, bring in a money partner. Share gains with someone else rather than chance wrestling with a fierce alligator.

Chapter Nine

Buyer Assistance Programs

Most people that are barely scraping by think that buying a home isn't even an option for them. But you won't get very far making assumptions about what you can and cannot afford until you look at the facts. There are tons of buyer assistance programs for first-time homeowners, and plenty for second-time buyers, too! Here are some of the best programs:

FHA Loans

An FHA loan is a mortgage insured by the Federal Housing Administration, a government agency within the U.S. Department of Housing and Urban Development. Borrowers with FHA loans pay for mortgage insurance, which protects the lender from a loss if the borrower defaults on the loan.

Because the loan is insured, lenders offer FHA loans at attractive interest rates and with less stringent qualifications. The FHA program was created in the 1930s as a responsive measure to the rash of foreclosures and defaults due to the Depression. The program was built to provide mortgage lenders with adequate insurance and to help stimulate the housing market by making loans accessible and affordable. Today, FHA loans are very popular, especially with first-time homebuyers.

FHA loans are one of the easier mortgage loans to qualify for because it requires a low down payment and less-than-perfect credit is okay. FHA requires a down payment of 3.5% of the house's purchase. Borrowers who can't afford the typical down payment of 20% or can't get approved for private mortgage insurances should look into whether an FHA loan is the best option for their personal scenario. Another advantage of the FHA loan is that it is *assumable*, which means if you want to sell your home, the buyer can *assume* the loan. This means, according to FHA.com:

Assumption of an FHA loan is a process where the responsibility of the mortgage is acquired by another person through "either Simple or Creditworthiness process."

The "Simple" assumption process is probably not useful to you since it is only allowed for FHA loans originated before December 1, 1986. Loans after that date may also be assumed, but the FHA requires a "creditworthiness assumption process." The "new" FHA rules require the borrower to qualify much in the same way he or she would qualify for any other FHA home loan. But, as noted above, it is generally one of the easiest loans to qualify for.

For more information see http://www.fha.com

CAL HFA - California Housing Financing Agency

The California Housing Financing Agency offers a variety of loan assistance programs to help buyers seeking residence in California. Most of them are tied to a first mortgage program- **CalPLUS Conventional and CalPLUS FHA**.

First Mortgage Programs:

There are many loans and programs built to help potential homebuyers find a loan. Many of them cater to first-time buyers, but there are many programs that do not have that inclusion. You might even think that since you've owned property before you don't qualify but in California, the definition of a first-time homebuyer is someone that has not owned a primary residence in the last 36 months. So, if you qualify by the definition (which you should verify with a lender or lawyer), you may qualify for some of the best loans available to California residents.

The **CalPLUS Conventional Loan Program** is for first-time buyers only. The interest rate is fixed throughout the 30-year term. The CalPlus Conventional Loan is combined with a **CalHFA Zero Interest Program (ZIP)** which is a second loan that covers the 3% down payment of the first mortgage loan. ZIP can be put towards down payment assistance or closing costs. First-time homebuyers can receive even more down payment assistance through **ZIP Extra**, which will provide an additional $6,500 of assistance at zero interest. This is the perfect solution for borrowers who have limited funds for a down payment or closing costs, but have the financial means to maintain monthly mortgage payments. Even though non-first-time homebuyers are not eligible for the ZIP Extra feature, they may continue to benefit from CalHFA's CalPLUS Conventional Loan with Zip.

The CalPLUS Conventional with ZIP Extra can also be combined with CalHFA's other assistance programs such as **CHDAP, ECTP,** and the **MCC** program.

Down Payment Assistance Programs
The **California Homebuyer's Down Payment Assistance Program (CHDAP)** provides a

deferred-payment junior loan up to 3% of the home purchase price, or appraised value, whichever is less, to be used for their down payment and/or closing costs.

The **Extra Credit Teacher Program (ECTP)** is a deferred payment, junior loan for eligible teachers, administrators, and classified employees and staff members working in county/continuation or high school priority schools in California.

With ETCP, you could receive a junior loan from $7,500-$15,000 depending on the area you are looking to buy. The loan can only be combined with an eligible CalHFA first mortgage loan. You must be a first-time buyer for this loan and occupy the property as a primary resident -- non-occupant and co-borrowers are not allowed.

Government Insured Loans

CalPLUS FHA Loan Program is an FHA-insured loan featuring a CalHFA fixed interest rate first mortgage. The loan is fully amortized for a 30-year term and is combined with the CalHFA ZIP for down payment assistance and/or closing costs. **This loan is not only for first-time homebuyers**, but second-time or more buyers can qualify if they meet all other conditions. First-time homebuyers can receive more down payment assistance through **ZIP Extra**.

Cal-EEM + Grant Program

The Cal-Eem + Grant program combines the FHA-insured Energy Efficient Mortgage first mortgage loan with an additional grant. This means that if you plan on making energy-efficient improvements to your home, you may qualify for this grant. The interest rate on the Cal-EEM is fixed throughout the 30-year term.

Other Partnership & Program Options
MCC

The Mortgage Credit Certificate is not assistance, but it will help you qualify for a loan. It is a dollar-for-dollar tax credit that covers 20% of your mortgage interest. The credit enables you to take 20% of total mortgage interest for the year and set it aside. You are then able to write off 80% when you deduct your net taxable income. The 20% pulled away is a dollar for dollar credit, which could be up to $2,000 a year. If you owe $2,000 at the end of the year you now owe nothing. This continues for as long as you live in the home.

Say that 20% of your mortgage interest is $2,000. Divide that by 12 (monthly) and it comes to $200. That's $200 more dollars in your pocket, which you can use towards your monthly mortgage payment, but are not required to. The certificate does not affect your mortgage payment, and saves you 20% interest.

Homebuyer Grants

A homebuyer grant is a grant that is equivalent to 5% of the first loan amount -- no lien, no interest, no payments required. If you qualify for your first mortgage there are three or four different programs in California. Some grants can be used for a down payment or closing costs. If you have 3% down on an FHA loan you can cover your entire down payment with a grant.

Individual Development Accounts:

IDA's are special savings accounts designed to assist low-income borrowers on their path toward ownership of a long-term asset, such as a home, through matched contributions by nonprofit organizations and eligible banks. These organizations may offer up to a 3:1 savings match (i.e. if you save $1,000, you will receive an additional $3,000).

To find an organization that offers an IDA program
see http://cfed.org/programs/idas/directory_search/
To find out more about all of the programs mentioned
above go to the CalHFA website
at: http://www.calhfa.ca.gov/index.htm

Chapter Ten

Selecting Your Team

There are potholes and pitfalls along the journey to success. The best way to avoid them is to be aware of what to look out for. From lousy realtors to money pit houses -- here are the ways to avoid making mistakes in your real estate investments.

Selecting a Realtor

I have been in this business for over 30 years. There are quite a few duds out there. Unfortunately, checking up on a real estate agent is not as easy as researching other service professionals. Most agents do not have a yelp page where people can publicly write a description of their service. They may have a Facebook page but even then they are likely to remove or hide any negative feedback that may hurt their business. The best way to get the 411 is to ask them to provide a list of what they've listed and sold in the past year with contact information. Before you begin calling names, ask the agent if anyone will be "particularly pleased or disappointed."

Ask the previous clients what the asking price was and then what the sales price was to see if the proof is in the numbers. Don't forget that every situation comes with its own limitations, but don't be afraid to be scrutinizing either. You ultimately want to hire someone you feel comfortable with, is a good communicator, and good listener.

Licensing

States have boards that license and discipline real estate agents in those states. Check with your state's regulatory body to find out if the person is licensed and if there have been any disciplinary actions or complaints, or check to see if the information is posted online.

For California residents, check the California Bureau of Real Estate at www2.dre.ca.gov/publicASP/pplinfo.asp to look up an agent or broker.

A poor agent could be the reason you do or do not get an amazing property. It pays to do the research. Just as doctors specialize, so do real estate agents. Ask what any acronyms listed in their email signature mean for example:

CRS (Certified Residential Specialist) -- Completed additional training in handling residential real estate

ABR (Accredited Buyer's Representative) -- Completed additional education in representing buyers in a transaction

SRES (Seniors Real Estate Specialist) -- Completed training aimed at helping buyers and sellers in the 50-plus age range.

If the realtor says he is a Realtor with the capital R, that means he is a member of the National Association of Realtors (NAR).

Experience

Be wary if they're new to the business. Many agents make mistakes as they learn the industry, and you don't want to be one of them. However, if their previous clients provide honest glowing reviews, and everything lines up, don't be afraid to take a leap.

Ultimately, you want to find someone who specializes in exactly what you're looking to buy. Familiarity with the neighborhoods you're interested in is important because then they will know local jurisdictions, schools, and price range. A good way to test if an agent knows an area is to ask about other houses for sale in the area. If an agent knows other properties and can give you a few details that means he really knows your area. You want someone like that who is on top of the market.

Online presence

Technology has drastically changed the real estate industry, and you want an agent who can use those tools effectively. An active online presence and attractive presentation on the Web is desirable because it shows knowledge of desirable business strategies.

Ask, ask, ask

Never be afraid to ask an agent a question. You're undertaking a huge investment and you want someone who has a great knowledge base and is willing to find the answers that he or she may not have.

Communication

Finding a good agent can be like finding a good job or a new relationship -- it needs to be a good fit. Communication is key. A lapse in communication for a few hours can mean the difference between an accepted offer and a missed opportunity. With that in mind, choose an agent that responds quickly in the mode of communication that works best for you, whether it's email, text, phone, or fax. Finding a realtor who will work with you in the way that you need is the best way to go.

Chapter Eleven

Finding a Home

Some people look for a beautiful place.
Others make a place beautiful. - Hazrat Inayat Khan

If home maintenance isn't a hobby or skill you learned growing up, you'll learn a whole lot in your real estate investing journey. Agents and real estate investors become well-versed in the structural makeup of houses simply just from coordinating home inspections, overseeing renovations, and exposure to a variety of homes. You may think it's not your job to know how a home works, but if and when you rent out a unit and YOUR tenants come calling to you because of a leak, then you will wish you knew more. Here are some of the most common problems that come up during home inspections and here is what to expect, what's normal, and what you should run away from.

Water is your enemy.

Water damage is one of the worst damages you can get. It's one of the most costly and dangerous --- causing foundation issues, rot, and the dreaded mold.

Signs that may indicate water problems:

Grade sloping (or draining) back toward the home) can be serious. Beware of any obvious opportunities for leakage like grade sloping. It could lead to wet crawlspaces, foundation movement, cracking or settlement. Water working its way through the foundation could lead to rot in the walls, creating structure instability and toxic mold. Some indications of foundation movement could be windows that are out of alignment, interior doors with large, uneven gaps when the door is closed, or floors visibly out of level. There can be multiple reasons for foundation movement so be sure to check what kind of problem it is. Many homes have quirks that can be manageable, but before signing on, keep on high alert and ask questions.

Roofing materials:

The roof is the structure that keeps the internal workings of the house dry. As the roof material ages, it lends itself to water intrusion and can lead to expensive repairs or even replacement. If roofing material is improperly installed, it can lead to premature aging. There are many types of roofing materials used to protect from the elements. The most common beginning with the most economical are: asphalt shingles, wood shakes/shingles/

terra cotta tile, concrete tiles, and slate. Ask the sellers what type of wood is being sold and look up its life expectancy. Asphalt shingles have a life expectancy between 15-40 years. Over time, the shingles will shift cup-shaped, forming up or down. Then the matrix (the material that holds the product together) will be exposed. This is when water becomes the most menacing threat to the structure. Make sure that you have the roof inspected. They are expensive and can be catastrophic if there is an internal issue. Look for moisture stains around the ceiling, walls, or windows, water ponding under or by the foundation.

Style versus Building Materials

When looking for your dream house, look for consistency in the architectural style and building materials. Rooms that appear to be added on can show an increase in functionality, but they can also show signs of unauthorized modifications and substandard workmanship. If, later on, down the road, you decide to remodel, you will be responsible with bringing these modifications up to code.

10 of the Most Common House Defects

1. Faulty wiring
2. Roof problems

3. Heating/cooling system defects

4. Plumbing issues

5. Inadequate insulation and ventilation in attic

6. Whole house is poorly maintained

7. Poor drainage

8. Air and water penetrating cracks and window perimeters

9. Minor structural damage – for example, attic cavities are magnets for cut and broken trusses which should be repaired but don't present a harsh threat

10. Potential environmental problems – ex. mold

How to Make the Most of Your Home Inspection

Consider Insured Inspectors

Everyone makes mistakes, even your home inspector, which can leave you footing a bill costing you thousands. When looking for a home inspector, choose an inspector who carries "Errors and Omissions" coverage. These policies go beyond basic liability insurance, and offer some level of protection if the inspector overlooks a damaged roof, or a furnace on its last legs.

Inspector Does Not a Repair Man Make

If your inspector notices something that should be repaired, he may take this opportunity to market his own handy work. This could also negatively affect your inspection. A home inspector who has been hired to repair defects may suddenly start noticing "defects" all over the home. The American Society of Home Inspectors even forbids its members from soliciting repair work based on the results of an inspection they performed. Beware of inspectors who offer their services for other tasks.

Home Inspection Does Not Cover Grounds

As the inspection states, a home inspection does not cover grounds surrounding the home, which can still give you a major headache. Keep your eyes open for issues with any outbuildings or fences. They may be expensive to repair, but a faulty fence does not necessarily mean imminent danger.

Home inspectors also don't inspect underground pipes, septic tanks, or wells, all of which are quite expensive to repair or replace. If you're looking to buy a large home that includes a number of outside features, negotiate these items into the inspection checklist. If your inspector is unwilling to cooperate or feels ill-equipped to handle these structures, consider hiring a second inspector who has experience in this field.

Double Check the Roof

Buying a home without seeing the roof can be a costly mistake. Home inspectors have no obligation to actually climb up and inspect the roof. Inspectors are expected to "observe" the roof, but there are no strict guidelines enforcing that the inspectors make a studied evaluation of its condition. To ensure that the roof is thoroughly inspected, confirm with the inspector ahead of time how he will check it out. You may offer to provide a ladder and assist as much as possible to provide safe and effective roof-access for the inspector.

What's Behind Your Walls

The biggest and most expensive home repair issues are often hidden away behind your walls. Rotted wood, or old wiring, can cost big bucks, yet even the best home inspectors probably won't find these problems because they are so internal.

A home inspection is a must before you finalize your home purchase. It is also a great safety net for you to have a professional weigh in on the property to ensure it is a good investment. Even though an inspection can catch some mistakes that the seller may be willing to cover, it does not guarantee that further problems will come up. Inspectors can miss some of the most expensive home issues because they're internal or for other reasons: plumbing, wiring, asbestos and lead are all serious issues that most inspectors miss.

There's not much more you can do to protect yourself without going into the walls of the house. This further illustrates the importance of saving a nest egg for home repairs.

Chapter Twelve

What Can Go Wrong

Every investment has some risk associated with it. In this chapter we will review areas that you need to investigate and strategize for to prevent any financial losses.

As the old adage goes, real estate is all about location, location, location. This is the most important criteria when selecting a property. It is imperative that you know the marketplace that you are considering buying in. Across the country there are real estate markets that consistently perform well. They range from large urban cities to smaller, mid-sized cities. The key to selecting the location is demand. Many things affect the demand for a property. One of the biggest desirable values is a view. The vicinity to water, whether it is an ocean, a lake or river, will create greater appeal and demand, therefore increasing the value. Properties at an elevation that provides views of city lights or the countryside also will help value them. Consider what will sell if and when you should decide to do so.

Another key factor to consider that should determine the location you will be investing in is the economy and the jobs available. People pursue cities with a good job market. If the jobs are drying up in a city, you will want to avoid it, because prices are sure to stall, or worse, and fall.

Consider the condition of a home that you are willing to accept. Are you in the market for a fixer upper or a pristine property? You will generally get your best value with a fixer property. However, you want to be sure that you know the full scope of the repairs. Cosmetic repairs are best because you get the biggest bang for your dollar with these repairs. They're generally inexpensive because they just visual and you will get a good return on an investment with an appealing style. Kitchens and bathrooms are generally the most vital when it comes to re-selling or renting a property. They are rooms that people spend a lot of time in and where the repairs appear the most expensive. Know what you're getting into when it comes to renovating these rooms.

Appliances and fixtures can also be incredibly expensive. Be sure to select materials that renters or buyers for re-sale will expect in that market. In other words, don't use high-end, expensive granite in a entry-level first-time buyer market because the buyers will never be able to pay the full market price for these products. Conversely, don't use cheap linoleum tile in a high-end community. It won't appeal to people interested in that market.

Cash Flow

Whether you are purchasing a new home and converting your current property to a rental or buying a rental property you want to be very careful about getting into a negative cash flow. Rental properties will invariably have unexpected expenses come up due to repairs or tenants. A positive cash flow will help with these expenses while a negative cash flow will only make this a bigger burden. If you are a high-income earner and have the disposable income and need the tax write off then it might be easy for you, but most do not have that luxury. Try to break even at least at the time of the purchase of the investment property and have your tenants cover the mortgage by offering reasonable rates for the property they are renting.

Tenants and Property Management

Dealing with tenants isn't for everyone. Some people love managing their properties and doing the repairs themselves while others hate it. The biggest key to investment property is having good tenants. Bad tenants can be a real headache with slow or no rent payments.

Abuse to the property and/or eviction are other areas of potential problems. The best way to prevent all of this is pre-qualifying the potential tenant in the same way that a lender would. Obtain a credit report: a person's credit is the best indicator of their character and commitment to their obligations. Paystubs and a reference call to a previous landlord are good ideas. If you don't want to deal with all of this then seek out a reputable property management company. (See in the next chapter for more instruction on becoming a landlord).

Market Timing

Purchasing real estate is best when it is part of a long-term investment strategy. But every investor wants to know about market timing so here are a few tips on when property values are near their peak and when there is room for an increase. In my experience, the most important factor in good real estate markets, as to whether prices are going up or not, is the affordability index. The real estate affordability index works a lot like a rubber band. When prices rise to a level that a shrinking percentage of consumers can afford to purchase a property in a certain market place, you know that top of that market is approaching. When only a small percentage of people can afford the current market price, then the pool of buyers reduces, therefore reducing demand. In a strong economy the Federal Reserve will generally raise rates, reducing affordability by design to slow the inflation rate on real estate. When the economy begins to stall the Fed Reserve will begin to lower rates to improve affordability, thereby increasing the pool of buyers. Savvy investors track the conditions and get in at these times. Ninety-nine percent of realtors and consumers are unaware of these market situations. Be aware and on top of this and you can do very well.

Chapter Thirteen

Lord of the Manor: How to be the best and smartest property owner

As a brother, a landlord, a master, she considered how many people's happiness were in his guardianship! How much of pleasure or pain it was in his power to bestow!

- Jane Austen

Renting out property and becoming a landlord is a huge undertaking with lots of responsibility. Not only are you responsible for tenant's safety and comfort, you have to come to terms with tenants who may complain a lot, don't pay rent, and unexpected immediate property repairs. These are all stressors that can be alleviated (or at least mitigated) with some calm consideration, and a fair approach.

It can be easy to start seeing tenants as dollar signs, instead of clients you're building a lasting relationship with. Creating a strong connection with your tenants, and marketing yourself as a great landlord, has numerous benefits. When things arise, having a good relationship with your tenant make everything from fixing repairs to showing the property to prospective new clients go much smoother, and your tenants are more likely to renew — possibly with a rent increase.

Here are some guidelines to help you be an excellent landlord that keeps tenants happy:

1. Customize the lease

You can get a standard lease form at any office supply store. These will cover basic things like rent, security deposit costs, and any legal tenant rights in your state. Use a basic lease as the framework for your own lease. Add in any special rules you have for the property, such as a weight limit on pets. Use as much detail as possible to include everything from late payment fees to maintenance responsibility and tenant's behavior. A clear-cut lease will reduce friction between you and your tenant in the future.

2. Know your stuff (the law)

Each state has a landlord and tenant act that covers rent, security deposits, landlord and tenant obligations, tenant's rights, and evictions. Get a copy, either online at the Department of Housing website for your state, or from the office in your area. Get to know the laws very well.

Violating a tenant's rights will, at the very least, lead to an unhappy tenant, and at worst, land you in civil court.

3. Make the repairs

When a tenant calls with repairs, set up a time to come and inspect the damage. If the repair doesn't qualify as an emergency, set up a time that works best for the tenant. Tenants will respect you, and appreciate your timeliness, if you let them know ahead of time when you plan to stop in, and many states require notice legally. Once you inspect the damage schedule a quick repair.

State laws handle property management maintenance differently. Some states allow a tenant to deduct repair costs from their rent, if you don't make them in a timely manner. Even if your state doesn't set a cap on repairs, the faster you make them, the better chance you have at retaining the tenant.

4. Keep communication open

While no one wants a tenant calling at all hours, it is important to keep the lines of communication open. Tenants feel more at ease when they know how to get in touch with their landlord, and when they respond. When a tenant moves in, give them your business number right away. Include an email address where they can reach you.

This will cut down on the amount of after-hours calls you get and help you keep a written record of communication between you and your tenants.

5. Listen to Your Tenant's Concerns

Every property management company deals with odd nosy neighbors, overly concerned tenants, or cranky complainers, but most tenants won't contact the landlord until they feel they have to. When you get a call from a tenant, listen to his concerns and do the best you can to make him feel like you addressed them.

6. Exercise compassion

At some point or another, tenants will have a problem. Maybe they're a day late on their rent payment, or they need to let a recently divorced friend sleep on the couch for a few weeks. Whatever the problem, try to tap into your compassion when dealing with their tenants, especially the good ones. If you show tenants a bit of compassion and let them slide on reasonable concerns/problems, they will remember the kindness. If tenants feel they have a compassionate landlord, they will be more likely to renew their lease or accept a small rent increase. Before you do anything, put the shoe on the other foot. Imagine how you would want to be treated, consider what is fair, and make a decision based on those considerations.

How to Find Great Tenants

"The essence of an investment in real estate is a good tenant. A good tenant in a bad location is better than a bad tenant in a good location." – James McClelland of property management firm Mack Cos in *MarketWatch*

It's an unfortunate reality: you can do all the right things and still end up with a bad tenant. You just can't know what's down the road for them whether it's a job loss, fighting couple, or good clean kids who partied harder than you thought. But here are ways to help you find the good tenants for the best possible outcome.

Follow the Fair Housing Rules

Read up on these rules to make sure you're not making tenant decisions based on race, gender, sex, religion, disability, or family status.

Tidy Up

Lazy landlords don't lift a finger before showing their property. Sweep up a little, make sure there are no essential repairs to be done, and add a fresh coat of paint once in a while. Generally, the cleaner and nicer the home is at move-in, the nicer it looks when the tenant leaves. Improvements attract strong tenants, and you may be able to charge more.

Meet Them in Person

This should go without saying. With all the various ways of finding tenants (i.e. CraigsList, RommateFinder, emailing through friends) it's easy to recruit them digitally. You want to physically meet them to make sure their story adds up and that you can have a conversation, show the property, and have confidence at lease signing that they will respectfully inhabit your property. The gut feeling you get from meeting a person is meaningful (so long as it's not being swayed by prejudices - see above note).

Check their references

This includes calling personal references, a past landlord, and or their employer. It may seem over the top, but it's very valuable that at least one reliable person is able to vouch for them. You'll want to have an actual conversation with these people. This helps you develop a better picture of what your tenant is like. Ask questions like: Did they pay rent on time? Did they have loud parties? Did they part amicably? If you don't do this, it could cost you thousands of dollars in repairs, and in the worst case, legal fees that were completely avoidable if you just made a simple phone call.

Perform a background check

Transunion's Smart Move is a great service for the landlord and the tenant. With this service your tenant is able to securely get a background check without you handling their social security number. And you can safely see if they are likely to be a good tenant.

Take a large deposit

Ask for a substantial deposit that will cover damages in case your tenant turns out to be a rotten apple. One key tip is to never make the deposit the same as their monthly rent obligation. Ask for more. Clarify if your deposit is "first and last month's rent, or just a security deposit." Make sure what their deposit covers is perfectly clear. This keeps it clear that they are accountable for their money.

Should you hire a property manager?

Buying rental property and becoming a landlord can be a very rewarding experience, despite the responsibilities it comes with. If you continue buying and renting out properties you may contemplate hiring a property management company. If that day comes, here are things to look for in a good management company:

Ask how many properties (units is the best term) they are managing

Ask how many employees are managing these units, so that you have an idea how much work is on their hands. A trained employee with the right tools and proven processes can manage between 30-40 units, assuming they don't operate accounting for each unit. If the company has way more units to employees, think about going elsewhere.

How will they overview the properties on a routine basis?

A critical component of managing properties and tenants is making sure the inspection is being handled respectfully. When you discuss inspections with prospective companies, ask for a commitment on how often they will conduct inspections of your properties. This may go over well with some managers. However, many will use this as an excuse to tack on a fee. Try to find one that has regular inspections (at a frequency you can accept) without an extra fee. Checking in on the unit is an essential part of renting, so if you're paying for someone else to manage it the service should be included.

Make sure they are strong communicators

Just like being a good landlord to your tenants, your property management company should be successful at listening to your concerns and responding with necessary courses of action. They are a middleman so it is essential to both parties that they are great listeners and communicators should any issues arise later. If conversations with managers are vague, divulge conflicting information, or simply short because they're cutting you off, watch out. They will treat you the same way later down the line.

See what's under the hood

You want to make sure that the property manager you select is using a quality property/tenant management tool (software) and that they can provide samples of output reports from this system during the interview. If they do not use software to improve efficiency or cannot give you a sample, you may be dealing with a company that offers slow services due to antiquity.

Ask how they charge

Most property managers charge somewhere between 7% and 10% of the total rents for managing your properties. Be sure that you know what the percentage is based on. Some managers will require that you pay them the agreed percentage on the total rents that COULD be collected, whether they are or not. Do not end up paying someone for rents that they did not collect.

How will they handle maintenance?

The best benefit of hiring a property management is knowing that if something goes wrong, someone else is able to check out the issue and take care of it without having to stress you out. That being said, you want to know the protocol for how the manager will resolve maintenance issues. They will want to make maintenance decisions up to a certain dollar value amount before they have to obtain your permission. Keep that payment low so that your permission is necessary before any heavy costs are charged.

Chapter Fourteen

Healthy Spending Habits

"Stop buying things you don't need to impress people you don't even like." – Suze Orman, financial writer

The process of building wealth has many levels to it, depending on how committed you are to the journey and how wealthy you want to become. These different levels include your personal psychology and self-discipline. These are both essential to your success as is what you do with the money that you save and invest. First, let's discuss one of the most crucial habits you must adapt to maintain the longevity of your success.

Saving is Essential to Being Wealthy

The key to becoming rich is to accumulate assets that will multiply in value. But not just any asset multiplies in value. There are two types of assets: appreciating and depreciating. Most people only buy depreciating assets -- things like cars, clothes, home goods, etc.. Appreciating assets arc investments like real estate, stocks, bonds, rare gems, stamps or coins, just to name a few. In order to acquire assets, you must save money to make investments. You know the old saying *You need money to make money?* It is very often true. In order to invest, you need to save enough money so that you build a sum that can purchase a desirable appreciating asset. So the first step to becoming rich is saving. **Your savings are your ticket to becoming wealthy.**

Unfortunately, approximately 50% of Americans have saved less than $35,000 during their lifetime. It is impossible to accumulate wealth without being able to save money. The number one mistake many people make in saving money is by setting a lifestyle first, then try to figure out how to pay for it. In other words, they select a home to live, a car to drive, buy clothes they like, then run out of money and begin borrowing on credit cards. This is a path that leads one place: bankruptcy.

One of the most common and debilitating habits is creating a poor budget plan. One thing I've learned about successful and unsuccessful financial planners is this: the unsuccessful ones prioritize savings at the bottom of the list. Successful ones pay themselves first. By putting savings at the bottom of the list there is very often only a little bit of leftover income that gets put into savings. This is like putting the pennies of change into an account and expecting it to grow. If this is hard to accept that you should prioritize your savings over the best cable available, take it from me: You will never become wealthy with a tiny savings account. Fatten it up.

The best way to build a good savings account is to save first, not last. A good start is to take 10% off the top of your earnings, but more will get you there faster. Put this into your savings account for investment. If you do not save first, you are very likely going to be unable to save much, and therefore will never be able to invest, resulting in a stagnant income and making it even harder to save for your own retirement.

Don't let spending squash your savings.

"Be thankful for what you have; you will end up having more. If you concentrate on what you don't have, you will never, ever have enough." – Oprah

As I mentioned in chapter two on belief systems, there are many people that will never reach financial wealth because of a negative belief system that holds them back. But let's say you don't have that challenge and are already established with a good job and earn good money. One might think that if this was the case there should be no problem rising to wealth, right? Wrong. The second biggest financial failure is pride. Why pride?

Overspending and maintaining appearances to keep up with the Jones's, as they say, is a huge problem.

Americans spend way too much on status items like clothes, cars, jewelry, purses, restaurants and entertainment. Do you shop based on brand names? Or do you do research to find discounts and good value for your money? If you chose the latter you are better off. It pays to shop smart!

High Rent = Higher Prices

Designer clothes and other status products like luxury cars can sap your money very quickly. When you need to purchase a product or service think about the location of the store or business you will be purchasing from. Merchants in high-rent cities have no choice but to charge a lot for the very same products that you can buy elsewhere because of their rent. A great example of this is in clothing stores. Shopping in a high-end mall for clothes will double or even triple for the same manufacturers that are located in an outlet mall. If you're thinking *Well, outlets sell last season's styles and I want the latest fashions,* think again. This is a major red flag indicating your spending habits are costly and unproductive, and will ultimately drive your financial success into the ground.. Spending more than you should on clothing shows a concern for status, and that is a pride problem that will continue to get in your way on your journey to wealth until you have it under control. The best thing for you to do is reconsider your value of status items.

This topic is one of the more controversial ones that I will address in this book and also one of the most essential. People simply don't want to hear not to overspend their hard earned money, but without getting this impulse under control, you will never be wealthy. There is an old saying, "money talks, wealth whispers." One thing I can assure you is that looking wealthy and being in debt is not nearly as fun as being wealthy and financially secure.

Learn from those who are wiser than you

When I opened up my own real estate business in the eighties, I worked long hours trying to build my contacts and make profits working at 8-11 hour days, but no matter how many hours I worked it seemed I was never where I wanted to be financially. This went on for years until I finally reached a place of complete frustration and realized there had to be a better way to help me reach my goals, and I needed help to find it. I began reading business books written by successful business people. I realized instead of suffering through the pains and stresses of costly mistakes I could read and learn them without having to go through all the pain and anguish personally. One of the most crucial lessons I learned at the get-go about building a business is to have a plan and create systems that carry out that plan.

Budget or Fail

You must have a structured disciplined system to budget and manage your money.

If you have a set salary that you can rely on each month it is easy to organize a plan. If your income varies each month because you work as a commissioned salesperson or are a small business owner, it can be more challenging because you are aiming for a moving target, so to speak. Regardless of your occupation, the first and most important step to becoming wealthy is to get in the habit of SAVING FIRST. Let me say that again, SAVE FIRST.

The best way to ensure that you will have money in the bank is to pay yourself first. If you are an employee with a company, set up a savings deduction of 10% off the top of your paycheck, you won't even notice it and your savings will grow effortlessly. If you are self-employed, transfer 10% of your income from every check that you withdraw from your business, and it put it in a separate, untouchable account.

Poor money managers select the nicer apartment, luxury car, and pointless trendy clothing to spend their money on, and soon realize there isn't any money left to save. This is an upside down and backwards thinking plan since it means that whatever is *left over* to go to savings, but unfortunately it becomes a habit to treat yourself to nice things without putting saving money aside, and your savings will likely dwindle. IF you want to truly become financially secure you must be able to accumulate and save the money you make. Saving is a priority if you want to begin investing to build *real* wealth.

Most people make the mistake of saving after all other expenses are paid for. The problem with this is that only a tiny amount of income is left. If you prioritize saving then you learn to be much more flexible around your budget.

Most people's budget plan looks something like this:

	N31	▼	=	
	A	B	C	
	\multicolumn{3}{c}{**MONTHLY BUDGET**}		

	ITEM	AMOUNT	COMMENTS
1			
2	ITEM	AMOUNT	COMMENTS
3			
4	Rent	$250.00	
5	Utilities	$50.00	Phone and Electric
6	Transportation	$220.00	Car payment, insurance, gas
7	Food	$200.00	
8	Medical Expenses	$35.00	Insurance contribution
9	Clothing	$75.00	
10	Leisure Activities	$80.00	Movies, dining out, etc.
11	Miscellaneous	$50.00	
12	TOTAL	960	
13			
14	INCOME	$1,225.00	
15	EXPENSES	$960.00	
16	SAVINGS	$265.00	

The savings are calculated last from whatever is left over.

This is the **wrong** way to budget.

My Monthly Budget

Category	Per Month Amount
Income	
My Salary	$5,200
Real Estate Income	$1,500
Total	$6,700
Expenses	
Investment Portfolio Contribution	$1,500
Emergency Fund Replenishment	$400
Savings Fund Contribution	$500
Rent	$2,200
Gas/Electric	$100
Sewage/Water/Trash	$50
TV/Internet	$75
Cell Phone	$100
Gas	$120
Car Insurance	$105
Groceries	$400
Eating Out	$500
Misc	$600
Total	$6,650

The **right** way to budget is to **SAVE FIRST.** Notice how this spender prioritizes saving for Emergency Funds and Savings. He considers it an essential expense- rather than a flexible left-over sum.

This budget plan includes two incomes and is probably more appropriate for a couple planning to have children. See how they incorporate the incomes and then calculate their savings to come directly from that income. If you put 10% of your paycheck into your savings consistently, you will see your savings grow and you will sleep much better knowing that you are planning for the future. It may be difficult at first and you might need to learn how to live a little differently. Here are some excellent tips to help make your dollar go farther, and to help you achieve your financial dreams.

When to Use Credit and When Not To

In the early 1980s I experienced my first recession. Because I earned my paycheck entirely on commission, I experienced a 50% income reduction. My income had been increasing at a rate of 25% a year for three consecutive years. The idea that it could drop so drastically never even occurred to me. Experiencing a 50% income reduction was extremely painful and difficult to say the least. During my first recession I learned that it wasn't the lack of income that was hurting me, it was my debt. I realized that if I didn't have any bills, an income reduction would not have been as big a problem. I needed my income to keep up with paying back debts, but if I didn't have those debts to pay I would have had a much less painful experience. After this experience I developed the mantra that *Debt is a four-letter word.* This has been a constant reminder to avoid debt at all costs and I've saved myself years of stress and have enjoyed many restful nights because of keeping my debts under tight control -- by having as little as possible.

How much should do you spend on interest?

Unsecure debt, which is debt that can go up and is without a fixed rate, such as credit cards, can, and usually do, have ridiculous interest rates. Some can be as high as 25% interest. The amount of interest costs alone that you can pay over a lifetime can be a real setback. NEVER finance anything with a credit card. Credit cards are great for the convenience factor and for tracking your expenditures, but using them as a way of financing a purchase over an extended time is a no-no.

Debt is a Four-Letter Word

Debt is a ball and chain. When you owe, you lose some of your financial freedom. You're no longer free to spend where you want, and it removes your ability to do things because you still owe the bank, and if you don't pay up it will severely hurt you and your future. The good news is there *is* such a good thing as good debt, compared to its evil counterpart, bad debt. Unfortunately, what you're probably staying up late and worried about is bad debt -- unnecessary debt that is causing you unhealthy stress and stopping you from accomplishing bigger purchases that will pay you back. Whether you are keeping up with the Jones's or just coveting what you see on television, it's time to lose the debt.

Since avoiding debt completely seems impossible these days, the best strategy is to borrow only to invest in assets (good debt), and avoid debts that don't help increase your net worth (bad debt).

My debt-reduction system:

1. Remove the temptation to spend. You have to learn to break the cycle of overspending and accumulating debt before it begins. For example, avoid your favorite "luxury" stores, and by luxury I mean unnecessary. Don't let material items lure you into purchasing an item you don't need. Go to your email newsletters and unsubscribe from promotional lists and coupon websites that will further trick you into spending on something you really don't need. This will be essential not only to putting money towards your debt and crushing it, but for when you begin saving smart for a mortgage. Adjust your lifestyle now, and save yourself from much worse pain later.

2. Get organized. You need to know who you owe, how much, the interest rates, and the regular payment. Once you know where you stand, you can execute the rest of the steps smoothly.

3. Negotiate your interest rates. Jesus said, "Ask and you shall receive." Let me tell you -- I've found that to be true, especially when it comes to dealing with banks. Sure, they're not giving handouts. But if you call to ask for a lower rate, and try to negotiate with them in a professional way, they are likely to consider. It doesn't take long either. Just call them up. If you're having difficulty, ask kindly for a higher up, a manager perhaps, that has more decision-making ability than the original person answering the phone.

4. Pay a little extra on the highest-interest debt. It will cost you the most. Cut back by a few drinks, or morning coffee runs each week so that you can pay more -- even $10 makes a difference. Once you've paid off the highest-interest debt, move on to the next.

Step 5: Don't incur more debt. Can you imagine denying yourself so many simply luxuries like a new shirt, pair of shoes, for months only to rack up that debt and have to do it all over again? It happens all the time. The most CRUCIAL thing you learn from ridding yourself of debt is to rein in your spending habits and make your dollar go farther.

One of my favorite quotes on saving is equally applicable to keeping the debt off:

"By definition, saving requires us to not get things now so that we can get bigger ones later."

-Jean Chatzky, financial editor for NBC's Today Show.

What about financing furniture and other home goods?

Another no-no. Furniture depreciates significantly right after you purchase it. My wife and I decided early in our marriage to buy antique furniture for a reason. Antiques are a nice way of saying *used furniture*. Additionally, like a vintage wine, antiques will never go out of style; if they've survived this far they've transitioned past the trendy years and into the classic.

Chapter Fifteen

Protect Your Investment

"It's not how much money you make, but how much money you keep, how hard it works for you, and how many generations you keep it for." - Robert Kiyosaki

How much home insurance do I need?

An essential part of successful investing is safeguarding your investment from unforeseen events. That's where insurance comes in. Homeowners insurance is a non-negotiable. It protects your home, its contents, and, indirectly, your other assets in the event of fires, theft, accidents or other disasters.

HO-3 Policy is Standard. What does it cover?

This standard homeowner's policy will protect you from things like fires and fallen trees. However, floods and earthquakes, and other natural disasters, are specifically not covered in standard policies and require additional coverage. In fact, homeowners in some parts of the country require their mortgage company to carry those policies.

A standard policy will also protect your possessions from said disaster, as well as theft. However, do not think of a standard as a blank check. There is a limit to how much you'll be compensated. If you have specific items of value, such as jewelry or artwork, you can pay a little extra every year to insure them for their full replacement value.

If someone trips and falls and sprains an ankle, they could sue you for their medical costs. A standard policy will cover liabilities like this.

How much coverage do I need?

Ideally, your home insurance policy would cover enough to entirely rebuild and furnish your home if it were wiped off the map. Ask a homebuilder to walk through your home and give you an estimate of what it would take to rebuild. The figure he gives you should be the basis for how much replacement coverage you'll need. Be sure to point out any specific or unique details that would add to the replacement cost. Once you've determined the replacement cost of your home, you'll need to know what kind of coverage you want.

Here are a few key terms to know when shopping for coverage:

Guaranteed Replacement Cost Coverage This means the insurer will pay for the rebuilding of your home no matter the cost. These policies can be hard to find, but do exist.

Extended Replacement Coverage

Many insurers offer coverage payout at around 125% of your home's insured value.

Inflation Guarantee (or Guard)

This feature protects the insured value of the home.

What should I get to be reasonably covered?

You will be in good shape with a reliable homebuilder's appraisal, extended replacement coverage, and an inflation guarantee. The appraisal will provide a realistic starting figure and the inflation guarantee will make sure your home's price stays current.

You've learned a bit about the negative effects of inflation. It applies to home reconstruction in the worst-case scenario that you need to rebuild. The 125% coverage protects you from that so even if construction prices outpace inflation you should still have enough money for whatever work you need done.

If you live in a high-risk area, it may be a law that you have flood insurance. To find out your flood risk and to find plans offered by the government, go to floodsmart.gov.

Valuables Coverage

If you have any possessions of particularly high value such as heirlooms, art, or jewelry, you may want to insure them. Insurers will charge extra for this coverage (approximately an extra $10 to your monthly premium per $1,000 of value insured).

Actual Cash Value vs Replacement Cost

Keep in mind the different types of coverage. Replacement Cost coverage is better for your valuables. Actual Cash Value is what you would get if you sold your valuable today – and likely a lower amount than what you initially paid. Replacement Cost Insurance pays you the amount of money you would need to buy a brand-new item to replace your old one.

Liability Coverage

If a guest gets injured and sues you, your homeowner's policy covers liability coverage in case you lose the court case. Generally speaking, standard policies offer $100,000 to $300,000 of liability coverage.

How to Shop for a Homeowners Policy

There are three different kinds of home insurance companies and salespeople:

1. Direct Sellers -- they sell directly to consumers (Geico, Progressive, and USAA fall into this group)

2. Captive agents -- they sell one company's insurance products (Allstate, State Farm)

3. Independent Insurance Agents – these agents sell policies from many different companies.

State Sponsored Insurance

If, for some reason, all of these groups reject your insurance application, there is another option. Many states have state-sponsored insurance programs for the hard-to-insure. Search for your state's FAIR (Fair Access to Insurance Requirements) plan if you're having a hard time with traditional insurers.

Home Insurance Deductible

Like auto or health insurance, your homeowners insurance has a deductible (the amount you must pay before coverage kicks in). If you want lower premiums (the monthly bill you pay) then opt for the highest deductible you can afford. A low deductible also forces your insurer to cover more of your costs, costs they pass on to you in the form of increased premiums.

Note: You should not use insurance to cover every conceivable expense, only the big ones. If reinstalling a gutter will cost you $200, pay the $200 -- don't start filing claims. Insurers dislike having a customer that files too many claims, and they may raise your monthly premium or even cancel coverage because they view you as too risky. Save insurance for issues like a whole new roof. The rule of thumb is this: If you can fix anything for less than $1,000, don't file a claim.

Legal Entities that Protect Your Real Estate Asset Wealth

If your real estate is not protected, you could be a lawsuit magnet. The law treats you, the property owner, as the guarantor for the safety of your tenants, employees, vendors, and anyone else who walks onto the property. Once you own investment property, you owe it to yourself to protect your best assets in case of unforeseen circumstances. We've already talked about insurance, but let's look at other legal opportunities to safeguard you from life's rainy days.

C-Corporation and S-Corporation

You can vest title of your real estate asset as a corporation, either a C-corporation or S-corporation. Both are formed by filing legal documents with the Secretary of

State. Both of these corporations are created as separate entities from the owners and therefore shield the owner or shareholder from personal liabilities. The S-corporation is the more commonly chosen corporation because shareholders are taxed directly and avoid the double taxation C-corporation brings.

LLC

A Limited Liability Company (LLC) is another great option for protecting your assets from legal trouble. An LLC also is formed by filing with the state. Owners of a corporation are called shareholders, while owners of an LLC are called members. The LLC also provides personal liability protection if filed correctly. The key ingredient in filing for an LLC is to elect to be taxed as an S-corporation to escape the self-employment tax imposed on an LLC.

Living Trust

A living trust does not require any legal filing with the State, but has the least amount of coverage if mishaps occur. Most people acquire a living trust to avoid probate and to carry out their wishes for how their estate is inherited. Many small business owners make the mistake of putting real estate property in joint ownership and elect not to form an LLC due to the perceived cost, effort and time associated.

But, as with anything that's worth time and money, it's wise to do this upfront work if you want the ability to protect your wealth.

What is the best option to protect my asset?

Your strongest legal entity is to vest title in an LLC and make sure it is appropriately insured. This means making sure the insurance coverage and policy amounts are adequate to your situation. When the LLC becomes the owner of a property, the LLC must be named the insured on the insurance policy. Failure to purchase and maintain adequate insurance could mean, in the situation of a lawsuit, that the court allows a prosecutor to pierce the company veil and hold the owner liable for the LLC's debts and liability responsibilities. This scenario leaves you vulnerable to expensive lawsuits.

Making smart legal decisions on your real estate investment allows you to get the most out of it now and for the future by protecting it. The unfortunate reality is that strong asset protection is extremely important for one simple reason: bad things that are out of your control can and do happen all the time. Protect your wealth and your investments by filing for a legal entity. It may save you a lot of money --and grief.

Conclusion

Why the Rich Stay Rich
and the Poor Stay Poor

Property investing is an arduous journey. Now that you have reached the end of this book you have gained (I hope) a knowledge base on the process of my wealth-building formula, smart strategies to finding the right rental property and how to rent it, and one of the most crucial elements to achieving success—the introduction to psychological obstacles you must overcome, whether you invest in property or not, to push your limits and accomplish your dreams.

Many successful get-rich-quick salesmen advertise "a deal of a lifetime." I am here not to preach about a miraculous deal- it's a lifestyle. One that will consistently bring in enough wealth to support your family, your retirement, and save you peace of mind for life. There will be ups and downs, as with everything, but if you strictly discipline yourself and your savings, you will be in position strong enough to withstand those storms.

Although market timing matters in your investments, building a solid foundation of knowledge, abilities, and entrepreneurial talents will be more valuable to you in the long run. As you gain experience you will develop market wisdom, and consistently find and know how to recognize, and even create, better opportunities. The "deal of a lifetime" is actually a "lifestyle" that can be adapted with patience and persistence.

The formula I have shared with you is succinct and simple, and yet builds wealth gradually and consistently. It doesn't take a miracle to be successful in real estate- it does however take determination, elbow grease, and incredible discipline. Changing your habits is extremely difficult but I believe it is possible to mitigate your mistakes and greatly increase your gains.

Buying into stocks, bonds, or social security, leaves your fate at risk. There is so little you can do to influence the returns you receive on those assets. Eldred reminds us in *Real Estate Investing* "Your financial goals mean nothing to stock markets, bond markets, or Congress. Not so with properties."

When you choose rental property as your opportunity for a lifetime of wealth-building, you can achieve good returns, even in a recession.

To profit from real estate requires due diligence, knowledge, effort, time, and market savvy. Unlike those who buy stocks, real property investors don't whimsically follow hot tips from Internet chat rooms, barbers, hair stylists, auto mechanics neighbors or the chatter of talking heads on cable tv. Smart and strategic real estate investors change their fates and control them even when surprises are thrown. They prepare for the best and the worst. Real estate provides a safer surer route to lifetime income and a comfortably secure net worth. Today, fanciful dreamers still believe that they and tens of millions of other Americans can achieve wealth without work. But dreams only come true with hard work, discipline, and determination and a smart playbook. So here is your playbook and go make your financial dreams come true.